If you've ever asked, "Why?" or "Why me, Lord?" you'll want to read this honest, hope-filled book, and share it with your friends.

    —Zig Ziglar, Ziglar Training Systems

Insightful, deep, and real, this book offers encouragement and hope through the best and worst of times.

    —Brenda Waggoner, counselor and author,
    The Velveteen Woman

The GRACE
of Catastrophe

When What You KNOW
About GOD Is All You Have

JAN WINEBRENNER

MOODY PUBLISHERS
CHICAGO

All Scripture quotations, unless otherwise indicated, are taken from the *Holy Bible, New International Version®*. NIV®. Copyright © 1973, 1978, 1984 by International Bible Society. Used by permission of Zondervan Publishing House. All rights reserved.

Scripture quotations marked NASB are taken from the *New American Standard Bible®*, Copyright © The Lockman Foundation 1960, 1962, 1963, 1968, 1971, 1972, 1973, 1975, 1977, 1995. Used by permission.

Scripture quotations marked THE MESSAGE are taken from *The Message* by Eugene H. Peterson, copyright © 1993, 1994, 1995, 1996, 2000, 2001, 2002. Used by permission of NavPress Publishing Group. All rights reserved.

Scripture quotations marked KJV are from the King James Version.

Library of Congress Cataloging-in-Publication Data

Winebrenner, Jan.
    The grace of catastrophe : when what you know about God is all you have / Jan Winebrenner.
        p. cm.
    Includes bibliographical references.
    ISBN-13: 978-0-8024-5041-8
    1. Suffering—Religious aspects—Christianity. 2. Theodicy.
I. Title.

BT732.7.W56 2005
248.8'6—dc22

2004027354

ISBN: 0-8024-5041-5
EAN/ISBN-13: 978-0-8024-5041-8

1 3 5 7 9 10 8 6 4 2

Printed in the United States of America

For all God's "wounded servants."

CONTENTS

ACKNOWLEDGMENTS

Mere thanks are inadequate, but let me try anyway, starting with all those brave followers of Jesus who told me their deeply personal stories of grace and catastrophe and gave me permision to share them. I couldn't have written this book if not for your courage to be transparent and authentic.

Thanks to the staff at Moody Publishers who caught my vision for this book and made working with them a pleasure.

And Karen Solem, my agent: Many thanks for those occasions you talked me down off the (writer's) ledge. You've always convinced me it's too soon to quit. You've always encouraged me to keep on keeping on. I'm grateful.

Thank you, Brenda Waggoner and Alan Elliott, for your critique and encouragement. Your friendship and expertise are invaluable.

My friends are too many to count. Margaret and Lynn,

what would I do without you? And Carolyn? Well, there are no words—or maybe you can suggest some?

Thank you, Grace Class, for being who you are.

Mom, thank you for being the first to encourage me to pick up a pen and write. Dad, thank you for telling me that "somebody's got to win the spelling bee . . .", and for believing it could be me. I am eternally grateful to God for both of you.

Only God could have known how much I would need my sisters, Susan and Paula. You've always been there for me, in every catastrophe, large or small. I thank God for you.

Thanks, too, to Matt and Jen and Molly and Jeff, for listening, reading, critiquing, sharing. Your wisdom belies your youth.

And the best for last: Thank you, Ken, for all you do to flesh out for me what Christ's love for His Bride, the Church, looks like. It just gets better and better.

GOD IS WHAT HE IS IN HIMSELF.
HE DOES NOT BECOME
WHAT WE BELIEVE. "I AM THAT I AM."
WE ARE ON SAFE GROUND ONLY
WHEN WE KNOW WHAT KIND OF GOD
HE IS AND ADJUST OUR ENTIRE
BEING TO THAT HOLY CONCEPT.[1]

A. W. TOZER

*I pray also that the eyes of your heart may be
enlightened in order that you may know the hope
to which he has called you, the riches of his glorious inheritance in the saints, and his incomparably
great power for us who believe.*

EPHESIANS 1:18–19

CHAPTER ONE

LIFE IN THE
MIDST OF MESS

Desperation makes us do strange things—things like sit up all night in a cheap motel and read the Bible out loud.

It's not something I'd usually do after a day on the road. On my best day, I'd probably watch a little TV, read a novel, then turn out the lights, and get to sleep early.

But let a catastrophe strike, and God has my attention.

Like the day my husband, Ken, and I set out on a cross-country move only to discover that the company transferring us to Texas had been sold. There was no job. That was the day we left town anyway—there was nothing to stay for. We were leaving behind an unsold house in South Carolina and heading toward one that the night before had just been flooded by torrential spring storms in Dallas. And so there we were: no job, two houses, and a truck full of furniture rolling along somewhere on Interstate 20.

That's the same day we were burglarized in the parking lot of a Holiday Inn on the outskirts of Atlanta.

Thugs now owned the few things we'd been reluctant to trust with the moving company, if they hadn't already discarded them in a Dumpster. Gone was Ken's wedding ring, his briefcase, our Bibles, clean clothes to change into, my special treasures, including six chapters and all my research and study notes for a book I was writing.

After doing an inventory and filing a police report, we climbed into the car and continued our journey west toward whatever fate awaited us.

I can't remember a time in my life when I felt more forlorn.

It's been a few years since that miserable, chaotic time in our lives, but it all seemed so recent when I read Charles Colson's words:

> Life isn't like a book. Life isn't logical or sensible or orderly. Life is a mess most of the time. And theology must be lived out in the midst of that mess.[2]

Looking back, our lives couldn't have been messier.

We had been stripped down to nothing in less than twenty-four hours. Our ideas about God were being challenged at the most basic level. That day, huddled together in a motel room in a Dallas suburb, we reached for the Gideon Bible in the drawer of a tacky nightstand.

We had nothing else to reach for.

The Most Important Question

That night we sat for a major exam in "Practical Theology." And the first question on the test: What do you *really* believe about God?

That's what catastrophe does for us, isn't it?

It forces us to confront our beliefs, maybe for the first time, maybe for the hundredth time.

It forces us to admit that maybe, when it comes to what we say we believe about God, we're frauds. It forces us to see where our trust really lies.

It forces us to face what we really believe we can expect from the God we call our Father.

All through that long night, Ken and I wrestled with these questions. We discarded what we thought were the wrong answers and pulled out what we thought were the right ones. And then, the next question loomed: How does that belief affect your life in this mess?

Which, of course, begs the next question: Does what you *say* you believe affect your life at all?

These were the questions that most needed answering —not, what will we do? Or, where will we live? Or, *how* will we live? And the answers would reveal the truth about us—if we really believed what we had for years claimed to believe; if the knowledge we held of God was biblically accurate, or false; if we were living authentic lives of faith.

What We Really Believe

A. W. Tozer wrote, "The difference between a great Christian life and any other kind lies in the quality of our religious concepts . . . i.e., what we think of God, what we believe about Him."[3]

Nothing so challenges us to examine what we believe about God like catastrophe.

> That our idea of God corresponds as nearly as
> possible to the true being of God is of immense
> importance to us. . . . Often only after an ordeal of

painful self-probing are we likely to discover
what we actually believe about God.[4]

We face difficulty, and we have to ask: Do we *really* believe God is strong and faithful? We face pain and illness, and we wonder: Is He as good as I've always been told to believe?

Death comes, and weeping, and we ask: Is heaven a reality?

Is prayer effective? Does God really hear?

The struggles and disasters of our lives prompt us to ask these questions, and dozens more.

Every tragedy, every crisis, offers us this:

> It can be a means of grace—an instrument used by
> God by which we can cease floating passively on all
> manner of external attractions. It is by the grace of
> catastrophe that people sometimes come to themselves and see what is before them as if for the first
> time. Catastrophe can, like a mighty wind, blow away
> the abstracting veils of theory and ideology and enable our own sovereign seeing.[5]
>
> —EUGENE PETERSON

It is the testimony of the ancients, as well as contemporary saints, that the greatest lessons of faith have been learned against the backdrop of suffering. The theology we say we believe takes root in soil watered by tears and bears fruit in lives characterized by peace and righteousness, lives that delight in the person of God Himself.

The "grace of catastrophe" comes through in places where our theology is tested, our faith forged, our knowledge of God made personal and practical, and our love for Him impassioned.

On the Brink

John Piper wrote, "Every moment in every circumstance we stand on the brink between the lure of idolatry and the delight of seeing and knowing God."[6]

Our stance is never more precarious than when we are in pain—any kind of pain. The voice of God whispers in our souls, "Love Me, worship Me, trust Me." But His soft words are hard to hear over the raucous voices in our culture and in our own hearts—voices that shout at us to berate God, to ignore Him and move on in search of other comforts, if there be any—any that don't wear off after a few minutes or hours.

Still, Jesus calls us to come close, to cuddle in His love and rest in the certainty of His goodness and His sovereign power. He invites us to take comfort in all that He has promised to be to us—savior, friend, healer, lover.

This is the challenge we face with each day as we step out into life.

Will we seek God and take our refuge in Him when our path is littered with broken dreams? Or will we turn elsewhere? We have only these two options when catastrophe strikes. If we choose God, then catastrophe becomes for us a special grace-gift, ushering us into the place where we can experience God in ways we never before imagined. We find ourselves poised on the brink of life's greatest discovery: that God is the ultimate presence in the universe, and that knowing Him, interacting with Him, by faith, is more satisfying, more exhilarating than anything the human heart ever hoped for or imagined.

Practical Theology

"What do unwounded servants do? They become arrogant, join country clubs, sell out to middle-class mediocrity. . . . Only the protected have the privilege of making theology a discussion; the endangered cling to it and weep."[7]

When we are wounded, hurting, crying in our pain, our theology—what we believe about God, about His kingdom—becomes suddenly very significant, very practical. We don't have the luxury of keeping it superficial. The truth of God's power and love and goodness, the truth of who we really are in Christ, the reality of His purposes for His people, the church, is suddenly relevant in ways we didn't consider in easier, more comfortable times.

We have no room for arrogance—the arrogance of certainty—when the unimaginable happens to us. Now, when our own souls are aching, we are suddenly haunted by the trite answers we so blithely tossed at others in their times of sorrow and fear.

It becomes painfully obvious to us—we don't have the privilege of making our theology a mere discussion. What we believe about God is now suddenly more important than anything else we will ever believe. It is more important than the doctor's opinion or second opinion. It is more important than a judge's ruling, more important than class rank, salary, retirement portfolio, or any of the other things that concern us in the course of our seventy- or eighty-odd years of life on this planet.

Theology, for the struggling disciple, is more than theory, more than a stimulating topic of discussion. It is more than the text of Sunday school curricula, more than the subject of a sermon. Theology is the truth that hauls us up out of the chaos and into the place of comfort in God's arms. It is the message that gives us courage to keep on living when everything in our lives seems to be decaying and deteriorating.

It is the truth of God, revealed in His Word, spoken in our hearts by His Spirit, lived in front of us by the incarnate Son that lifts us up. Without it, "we remain little people with little concerns who live little lives and die little deaths."[8]

Grace in Doubt

Since that messy, frightening arrival in Texas, I have faced many other obstacles, many that were much more painful, much more life altering than a job crisis and a real estate deal gone sour and the loss of a few material goods. I've had to retake that exam on "Practical Theology," and many times, I've failed.

I've doubted that God is really good.

I've wanted to curse, not sit and read Psalms.

I've refused to pray, because in those moments of greatest agony, I wasn't certain that God would hear and answer, that He could be trusted with my pain.

I've wondered, *really* wondered, if there is a plan to all the chaos. I've doubted if God was going to come through for me.

In my worst moments, I've wondered if He cares, if He loves. And I still, at times, wonder if He is really as good as He says He is, as good as I need Him to be.

I've said with David the psalmist, "Why, O LORD, do you stand far off? Why do you hide yourself in times of trouble?" (10:1).

Will you forget me forever?
How long will you hide your face from me?

How long must I wrestle with my thoughts
and every day have sorrow in my heart?
How long will my enemy triumph over me?
—PSALM 13:1–2

You've probably echoed David's sentiment. You've felt the pain of loss and the desolation of loneliness. You've struggled to believe the truth and wondered if maybe, just maybe, you've gotten it all wrong. But have you ever echoed these words of David?

I trust in your unfailing love;
My heart rejoices in your salvation.
—PSALM 13:5

I will praise the LORD, who counsels me;
even at night my heart instructs me.
—PSALM 16:7

David, grubbing for food in the desert, sleeping in a cave with vagabond mercenaries, fighting for his life, discovered that grace could be found in unlikely places. God Himself counseled him in moments of confusion. Listen to his testimony: "You have made known to me the path of life; you fill me with joy in your presence, with eternal pleasures at your right hand" (Psalm 16:11).

A Gift of Opportunity

Catastrophes come to all of us, in forms too numerous to count. But with every catastrophe comes this gift—the opportunity to see God at work in our lives, on our behalf; the gift of opportunity to experience what we say we believe—about God, about His kingdom, about His people.

It is through the grace of catastrophe that we begin to experience the theology that, for most of us, is too often relegated to the academic, the theoretical, realms of our existence. By the grace of catastrophe, we are offered the opportunity to enter into our theology, humbly, and with great anticipation. We are gifted with the chance to experience God in ways we never before imagined, nor hoped for.

John Bunyan wrote, "Let it rain, let it blow, let it thunder, let it light[ning], a Christian must still believe."[9]

The thunderbolts reverberate from every corner of the world, it seems. The echoes of suicide bombs shake us in the depths of our souls. The sounds of gunfire in our world, in our cities, in our own communities, send us in search of shelter, if there be any. The Internet brings us images of beheadings, images of torture and ignominy. Our hearts reel at the kind of catastrophes that greet us in the morning paper—and this before we've had our first cup of coffee, before the phone rings with news of a family crisis, a job crisis, before we've had a chance to enter the fray of our own chaos—kids, jobs, road rage. Everywhere we turn there is catastrophe on some level. Everywhere we turn there is the challenge to believe.

We must still believe that God is who He says He is; that He is as good as we hope and pray He is; that His kingdom purposes will prevail, regardless of the storms that encircle our world.

The Christian must still believe—theology must be lived out in the midst of whatever mess we might find ourselves: the international/global kind that makes the evening news, as well as the interpersonal ones that greet us when the kids climb out of bed in the morning, when the boss walks into the office with less-than-good news, when the car engine refuses to turn over, when the medical tests reveal something awful, when the parent/teacher meeting is negative.

When life happens, we must still believe.

We must hold on to the truth.

And as we deliberately choose to hold on to the truth, which is holding on to God Himself, we discover His presence to be more loving and tender, more astoundingly personal than ever before, and catastrophes become for us a means of grace—a means of knowing and delighting in God.

Tracking Grace

But what does it look like to "hold on to" an invisible God?

Can our fingers actually grip His hand? Can we wrap ourselves in the warmth of His regal garments?

Years ago I discovered that I could hold on to God through pen and paper. It was my mother's suggestion to me when I was a young mother of two, struggling to stay a few steps ahead of despair. Ken was traveling heavily, my children were babies, and I was lonely, weary, and battling a growing cancer of bitterness. Every day held its own catastrophe—whether an emergency visit to the pediatrician for a shot that would enable Molly to breathe, or a broken air conditioner on a summer day when the temperature soared to 113 degrees (we lived in Phoenix).

Mom visited me one day when I was especially haggard. She could do little to help out because she had her own crises to deal with at the time, but what she offered that day changed the complexion of my spiritual life.

"Honey, why don't you keep a notebook with your Bible and try writing down how God is dealing with you? Write down verses that mean a lot, the ones that encourage you, and keep a record of God's faithfulness."

No one else was offering me a remedy for peace that day, so I did what she suggested. I bought a notebook the size of my Bible and my life of faith has never been the same.

I began by rewriting passages from Psalms, putting them in language and metaphor that I could connect with. Later I began shaping them into poems. Often having only snippets of time, I wrote verses on scraps of paper, carried them in my pockets or stuffed them in the cup holder of my car and memorized them while my hands were busy with other things. Later I played with them in a notebook, writing and rewriting them, squeezing every ounce of truth and meaning out of them.

Now, looking back over nearly thirty years, I can see that this has been my means of holding on to truth and leaving markers—markers that still stand as monuments to God's goodness, love, and faithfulness.

I have been tracking grace.

In her book *The God Hunt*, Karen Mains calls it keeping a "life list," keeping a record of "divine activity":

> These are not mundane accounts. . . . They have to do with the Creator of the universe chasing after me in crazy love so that his nearness, his closeness, his within-ness can be recognized and known by me.[10]

Call it journaling, call it your "life list." Call it whatever you like, but for me it is the tracking of grace.

Paul closed the book of Philippians with this encouragement to the Christians he loved: "Receive and experience the amazing grace of the Master, Jesus Christ, deep, deep within yourselves" (4:23 THE MESSAGE).

Somehow, that grace seems to plow deeper into my soul when it has been moistened with tears and softened by suffering. Its tracks are more visible. And always, those tracks lead to greater knowledge of God, greater intimacy, and a kind of deep interior joy that can't be touched by circumstances, or catastrophes—large or small.

The Path to Joy

I hope as you read and study about the character of God and His kingdom, you will grab a pen and "track grace" in your own life. I hope and pray you will anchor it in ink.

I hope you will recognize, in that moment when pain pierces, or when the weight of life presses on your chest until it hurts to breathe, that hiding from God isn't the answer. That running away is not the way to go.

I hope you will run *to God*. That you'll open His Word and read and listen, with a pencil in hand. I pray that as you write what you hear and what the Holy Spirit makes known to you, you will sense truth being traced on your soul—that you will recognize the indelible mark of grace. I pray that the reality of God's unfathomable love will imprint itself on your heart and that you will experience His powerful presence in new and wonderful ways.

I pray that whatever catastrophe, large or small, you encounter today or tomorrow will cause you to hold on to truth, to cling to God Himself.

As you cling, may you develop a record of His grace, tracking your own path to intimacy and joy.

And in those tracks, may you see the nail-scarred footprints of Jesus your maker who, for "crazy love," is chasing after you.

TRACKING GRACE

IF WE COME TO BELIEVE THE WRONG THINGS ABOUT GOD,
WE WILL THINK THE WRONG THINGS ABOUT OURSELVES,
AND WE WILL LIVE MEANLY OR BADLY.
TELLING A PERSON A LIE ABOUT GOD DISTORTS
REALITY, PERVERTS LIFE AND DAMAGES
ALL THE PROCESSES OF LIVING.[11]

—EUGENE PETERSON

Jesus said, "If you hold to my teaching, you are really my disciples. Then you will know the truth, and the truth will set you free."

—JOHN 8:31–32

1. Write a description of God as you believe Him to be. Be honest.

2. Describe the kind of relationship you could have with the God you've described.

3. Thinking about the most recent catastrophe you've experienced, what did you expect from God, if anything?

4. Read Psalm 9:10. Write your response. Now, try writing the verse in your own words, keeping in mind that trust can also be understood as "to be attached to," "to be secured," or "to have expectations."

5. Write a prayer to God, or a poem, based on Psalm 9:10.

GOD'S WRITTEN WORD
IS FULL OF MYSTERY;
HIS WORD ACCOMPLISHED
ON EARTH IS NONE THE LESS SO.[1]

JEAN-PIERRE DE CAUSSADE

As you do not know the path of the wind,
or how the body is formed in a mother's womb,
so you cannot understand the work of God,
the Maker of all things.

—ECCLESIASTES 11:5

CHAPTER TWO

God's Unfathomable Ways

THE THEOLOGY
OF TRANSCENDENCE

Jim Davidson is a surgeon among surgeons. Voted by his peers in the medical community as one of the Dallas/ Fort Worth "Top Docs," he has a busy practice as a vascular surgeon. But not too busy to serve with a mission team on a hospital ship that cruises the Amazon River for ten days every year, anchoring near the shore of tiny jungle villages to serve the natives, many of whom have never seen a doctor. This year, his wife, my good friend Carolyn, who was a nurse for many years, went along to assist him.

The first day on the river, while organizing and stacking medical supplies, Jim fell five feet into the ship's hold, landing on his back, fracturing his right scapula and slicing a chunk out of his left thumb. He went into shock twice before he could be airlifted out by float plane and taken to a hospital in the nearest city of any size.

The mission team was heartbroken. They all had

learned to love Jim over the many years he had traveled and ministered with them. A tireless worker, he operated ten to twelve hours every day, repairing every kind of condition curable by surgery. Often, he was the only doctor the villagers along the Amazon River would ever see in their lifetime.

"Why, Lord?"

Before he could operate even once, or treat even one patient, Jim was on his way back to Dallas, with Carolyn, leaving the team without a doctor for the remainder of their journey down the river.

Carolyn called me after she and Jim arrived home.

"I know God has a plan, although we may never know it. It does seem senseless."

She was thinking of all the children with cleft palates —children ostracized, discarded by their families, left to die in alleys because they are ugly and difficult to feed and care for. Under Jim's scalpel, they were given new lives, new hope. Often, within hours of corrective surgery, they were welcomed back into their families. Seeing their faces, knowing how life will improve for them—it was a highlight of the medical journey.

Carolyn said it again, "We'll probably never know what it is in this lifetime, but I know God has a plan."

Carolyn is a woman who has grabbed hold of the theology of transcendence.

Embracing Transcendence

The theology of transcendence says that God is infinite, and our finite minds cannot grasp all that He is, all that He wants to be to us, all that He is doing, and all that He wants to do for us. We are incapable of fully plumbing the depths of God, His character, His plans, His goals; nor can we completely comprehend the strength of His love, the passion of His pursuit of us, the lengths to which He will go to make Himself known to us.

He says of Himself:

> *"My thoughts are not your thoughts,*
> *nor are your ways My ways," declares the Lord.*
> *"For as the heavens are higher than the earth,*
> *so are My ways higher than your ways*
> *and My thoughts than your thoughts."*
>
> —ISAIAH 55:8–9 NASB

David cries out, "Among the gods there is none like you, O LORD; no deeds can compare with yours" (Psalm 86:8).

All that God is, all that He does, has done, and will do, surpasses what our finite imaginations can conceive. He is like no other being. Whatever we can imagine about God is too small to do justice to His infinite person.

Whatever is occurring in my life, whether good and joyous, or painful and distressing, is a part of a larger story, an ongoing drama that reaches from eternity to eternity.

In short, the theology of transcendence teaches that there is a bigger picture than what our senses can discern. There is a "larger scene where love rules."[2]

The longer I live, the more I study, the more convinced I become that all I know and experience must be considered in the context of God's transcendence.

The Larger Scene

Nothing helps us see that there is a larger scene than the story of Job. Wealthy, devout, and content with his life, Job is struck suddenly with incalculable losses. His children killed, his servants murdered, his wealth ransacked, and his health in tatters, he finds himself in unutterable pain. All that is left to him is his wife who is as heartbroken and devastated as he is. Showing up on the scene, recently arrived with the latest caravan, are Job's friends, who are appalled at what has happened to this fine, upstanding citizen who never wished anyone any harm. They are at a loss to explain what has happened to Job. But, undeterred, they try anyway.

I see myself in this ancient drama. It doesn't matter than I am a twenty-first-century woman, I could be any one of these characters. I have been a victim of disaster and a commiserating friend. I have been both shrewish wife and suffering saint. Like Job and his cronies, I have spent long hours trying to figure out what happened. What went wrong? What did I do to deserve this thrashing at the hands of God?

I have watched my friends and family suffer horrible losses and physical pain, and I've wondered, what did *they* do that prompted God to unleash such chaos into *their* lives?

Occasionally, one can see the cause and effect. A friend with a two-pack-a-day habit suffers from cancer. Repeated surgeries have left their scars, yet she refuses to quit smoking. I learned recently of a family who lost their business and home because of a father's gambling habit. In the "blame game," these are no-brainers.

But most of the time, there are no easy answers. Often, there are no answers at all. We stew in confusion and shout our "whys."

Even the greatest minds have to finally say that there are mysteries that elude our ability to comprehend. To insist on full understanding is nothing but futility.

"It is the logician who seeks to get the heavens into his head," wrote G. K. Chesterton. "And it is his head that splits."[3]

If ever heads were splitting with the effort to figure out the heavens, it was there in the land of Uz. Against a scene of unthinkable suffering, finite minds were trying to explain the infinite mind of God and analyze His actions.

At first, speechless in the presence of such intense agony, Job's friends simply sat with him and wept with him. Then, finally, they began speculating on the reasons for Job's horrors. One by one, they explained in great detail what Job had done to deserve God's punishment.

In Job chapter 4, Eliphaz tells Job he has brought this on himself and he needs to admit it. You're not so perfect, Job, he's saying. "God . . . doesn't even cheer his angels, so how much less these bodies composed of mud, fragile as moths?"[4]

In chapter 8, Bildad blames Job's kids—this is all their fault.

Chapter 11: Zophar, good friend that he was, scolded Job—get it together, buddy; clean up your act.

By chapter 34, Elihu, the young upstart of the gang, who has listened to the old-timers for a while and can't stand it any longer, finally puts in his two cents' worth: Somewhere along the way, Job blew it, and now he has to pay for it.

I've sat in on similar conversations, haven't you? I've been both a participant and the subject of them. And these words from Michael Yaconelli's book *Dangerous Wonder* convict me. He wrote, "The Church should be full of Christians who seek questions rather than answers, mystery instead of solutions, wonder instead of explanations."[5]

Amy Carmichael wrote, "Absolutely refuse the natural human point of view where trial is concerned."[6]

If ever a woman had opportunity to ponder her troubles and question God, it would be Amy Carmichael. She spent twenty years, the final quarter of her life, confined to bed, injured and in constant pain, almost immobile after a terrible fall. The woman who had so passionately served God as a missionary in India, rescuing infants and children abandoned in pagan temples for use as prostitutes, was now, herself, almost as helpless as the orphaned children she loved and cared for at Dohnavur Fellowship.

The human point of view might have offered dozens of explanations for Amy's injury. Was she inept at leading? Was God punishing her for some infraction, some failure in service? And because she was human, and spoke and wrote often of her weakness and spiritual battles, we know she fought hard to refuse that point of view. We know she fell back on the theology of His transcendence. She wrote this:

> Out of my vision swims the untracked star,
> Thy counsels too are high and very far,
> Only I know, God of the nebulae,
> It is enough to hold me fast by Thee.[7]

The natural human point of view fails miserably to explain our sufferings. Yet wonder seeking is not a common activity within the church, is it? Oh, on that rare occasion we might sit and ponder the idea of a magnificent mystery, just beyond our vision, but too often we are preoccupied with plotting, not pondering. Our souls are not moved by the powerful force of mystery. Our imaginations are not dazzled by divine possibilities.

And so we analyze and seek reasonable explanations for suffering.

A first-time visitor to a women's Bible study shared that her child was in the middle of a nasty divorce. A woman sitting nearby commented, "Since the day she was born, I've prayed every day that my child will marry a

Christian and have a strong marriage." The inference, of course, was that the visitor *hadn't* prayed for her child every day—and now look at the mess she was facing.

Parents of a drug-addicted teen talked with me at church one Sunday about their heartbreak. They were only hours away from a kind of intervention program that would put their child in a "boot camp" for treatment—one more attempt in a long series of efforts to help this child they loved more than their own lives.

"We've heard it all," they told me. "The critics have studied us, analyzed us, hoping to see some obvious error in our parenting so they could avoid making the same mistakes. Some said we didn't love enough, some said we loved too much. Some said we didn't discipline enough, others thought we'd been too tough."

The censure lay heavy on the shoulders of those godly, bewildered parents who were desperate for answers themselves. While they agonized, others adjusted their behavior in opposite ways, wrapping themselves in a cloak of certainty about the dos and don'ts of parenting.

Dallas Willard wrote, "One's feeling of righteousness does not mean he is right and actually should alert him to be very cautious and humble."[8]

Humility doesn't often describe our responses to another's suffering, does it? It is tempting, almost irresistible, to judge and make assumptions about circumstances, causes, consequences, especially when it comes to family issues. I confess, my thoughts often start to travel that road, and then the words from Ruth Bell Graham's poem prick my heart: "Remind them gently, Lord, You have trouble with Your children too."[9]

We want desperately to be able to find reasons for catastrophe, don't we? Our thinking follows this route: If we can just find specific actions that can be taken to deter catastrophe, maybe we can live diligently enough to secure our safety, and the safety of those we love. But most of the sorrows we encounter leave us baffled and asking "Why?"

After we've listened to the rationalizations of well-meaning friends, and mulled over our own flawed explanations, we've probably encountered a few pious-sounding folks who scolded us for questioning God's dealings with us at all. And our misery multiplies.

Here is where we pick up Job's story again.

"Why?" Yields to "Who?"

After all the whys had been asked, after every explanation had failed to bring light and assuage Job's pain, after his friends' voices fell silent, God Himself addressed Job.

"Why?" yielded WHO.

God spoke:

Where were you when I created the earth?. . .
Who decided on its size?. . .
Who came up with the blueprints and measurements?
How was its foundation poured,
and who set the cornerstone,
while the morning stars sang in chorus
and all the angels shouted praise?
And who took charge of the ocean
when it gushed forth like a baby from the womb?
That was me!
I wrapped it in soft clouds
and tucked it in safely at night.
Then I made a playpen for it,
a strong playpen so it couldn't run loose,
and said, "Stay here, this is your place.
Your wild tantrums are confined to this place."

Can you catch the eye of the beautiful Pleiades sisters,
or distract Orion from his hunt?
Can you get Venus to look your way,
or get the Great Bear and her cubs to come out and play?
Do you know the first thing about the sky's constellations
and how they affect things on Earth?
Can you get the attention of the clouds,
and commission a shower of rain?
Can you take charge of the lightning bolts
and have them report to you for orders?

—JOB 38:4–11, 31–35 THE MESSAGE

"Here I am," God said. "*This* is who I am."

In the midst of Job's pain and confusion, God thrust on him this astounding facet of the divine nature: God's majestic supremacy; His transcendence over everything that ever existed or ever will exist.

Job's response: "I admit I once lived by rumors of you; now I have it all firsthand—from my own eyes and ears! I'm sorry—forgive me. I'll never do that again, I promise! I'll never again live on crusts of hearsay, crumbs of rumor" (42:5–6 THE MESSAGE).

And Job fell on his face and worshiped God.

Job learned this: that unless we know that God is transcendent, anything else we believe about Him will be inaccurate.

This is the truth we must discover for ourselves: that the God presented in the Bible is above us, beyond our understanding, that He surpasses every idea we've ever had of Him; that any idea or thought we have of God, any tradition passed from generation to generation, any belief, any concept of God is less than He is.

Rumors and "crusts of hearsay" cannot come close to accurately describing the immensity of God's infinite person.

No matter how high our expectation may be,
when God finally moves into the field of our
spiritual awareness we are sure to be astonished
by His power to overwhelm the mind and fascinate
the soul. He is always more wonderful than we
anticipate, and more blessed and marvelous than
we imagined He could be.[10]

—A. W. TOZER

Job, astonished, overwhelmed, fascinated, whispered, "I'm speechless, in awe—words fail me" (40:4 THE MESSAGE).

He bowed and worshiped in "delighted wonder" willing to relinquish the pursuit of "why."[11]

Job's story amazes me. Chapter after chapter, verse after verse contain declarations of what God is like—some of it accurate, some of it horribly mistaken. Passage after passage show us Job's lament, his sorrow, his suffering, his confusion. Then, finally, after all the worst has happened to him, when Job has nothing left to lose except the breath in his chest, God answers him.

Don't miss this important fact: Even though God didn't tell Job why, He *did* speak to Job.

Job discovered, through his catastrophic experiences, that God is not like he had imagined. God does not desire ritualistic sacrifices, impersonally offered for vague, unknown infractions. God does not capriciously bless nor casually curse His creation. God does not behave according to human expectations, nor does He require Himself to respond to every human demand.

The God of Job was unlike the gods of his neighbors —images made of wood and stone, chiseled out of marble and plated with silver and gold, elements that could be handled or whittled, formed, controlled, and owned.

This God whom Job worshiped refused to offer reasons or apologies. Yet, He would introduce Himself. He would *speak*.

Transcendent, superior, above and beyond all human artists' conjuring, God revealed Himself on the intimate level of conversation. His voice like a wind, He stirred the ground and wrapped Himself in dust to speak. And Job was never the same.

The Word Becomes Flesh

Centuries later, God would once again break into the silence of human suffering. Four hundred years after the last prophet had been heard, God would speak. The Word would become flesh.

Wrapping Himself in a body like that of the first man formed from the dust of earth, God the Son, the Word, came to live among us to let us behold the glory of God. To let us get to know Him—incarnate God, exposed, wearing muscle and bone and sinew.

"This is who I am," Jesus said.

"Anyone who has seen me has seen the Father" (John 14:9).

"I and the Father are one" (John 10:30).

During His last evening with His friends, Jesus told them, "Be prepared. Trouble awaits you" (see John 16:33).

And then, He added, "But don't be afraid, because I have overcome your trouble."

I am transcendent.

I am over all things and above all things.

Hours later, the greatest catastrophe of all shook the universe, from galaxy to galaxy. The unimaginable oc-curred: God the Son, clothed in humanity, crucified by an angry mob, intent on silencing the message that contra-dicted their lives and shamed their worship.

What they couldn't see was the bigger picture—the truth that transcended their cruelty. In the unfathomable horror of the cross, lay the inconceivable depths of God's love. Against the pain and desolation of the crucifixion, lay the truth of redemption.

This is truth that boggles our minds: God in love with us, pursuing us, going to the greatest of all lengths to rescue us and restore us.

Beyond All Expectation

Millie Stamm wrote, "Faith expects from God what is beyond all expectation."[12]

That is the definition of transcendence that the Christian clings to. Beyond our understanding, yes, and beyond all expectation, He is "the One who unimaginably transcends the worst things as He also unimaginably transcends the best."[13]

When pain settles around my heart, when "Why" pounds loudly, I think of Job's seeking. I think of God's response: He answered. He disclosed *Himself* to Job, if not His purposes and His reasons. And the disclosure was enough for Job. It brought him to his knees. It quieted all questions. It satisfied him.

This is the truth that startles our human souls: When we encounter God, in His transcendent glory, nothing else matters. Hearing His voice, actually experiencing communion with Him, removes all other yearnings—for answers, for explanations, for anything but God Himself. We don't expect this. We don't even know we want it! But when catastrophe has cut us off from all other comfort, and when God Himself enters our experience, His transcendent majesty dwarfs all other comforts, His voice silences all other voices, and His love overwhelms all other loves. We find out, for the first time in our lives, that it is God who we want. It is God who we crave and desire; it is only God who can satisfy us.

In his book *Desiring God*, John Piper says it over and over again, "God is most glorified in us when we are most satisfied in Him."[14]

That is the place where we find Job in the final words of his story. His children are dead, his wealth is lost, his body is weak, and his wife angry; but the only thing that matters to him is God's presence. He heard God speak and was satisfied.

Worth the Cost

No writer can adequately describe the sense of fullness and wholeness and satisfaction that settles into the soul when God has made Himself known, but John Piper's epic poem, *The Misery of Job and the Mercy of God*, comes close. In the final pages of verse, Job is speaking with a daughter born to him after the loss of his first family. He is trying to explain to her what happened in his life before her birth. Her questions about the comments of his old friends prompt him to answer:

> You see, their minds were small,
> And they could not see painful times
> Apart from dark and hidden crimes.[15]

Warning her, this daughter born in his old age, he tells her, "Beware, Jemima, God is kind, in ways that will not fit your mind."

It's true. God's ways of being kind do not always fit our minds. Because He is transcendent—larger, higher, far more holy and incomprehensible than we will ever be able to wrap our brains around.

We can't really grasp the infinite love and wisdom that compel His dealings with us. And when we have been dealt with by God, on His terms, in mysterious, wondrous ways, we find ourselves at a loss to express the richness of the deposit He has made in our souls.

Words fail me as I try to tell about the first time I really experienced the presence of God. It was in the wake of bitter disappointment. One moment I was mourning over shattered dreams, in the next, I heard the voice of God whisper in my soul, "It's going to be okay, Jan."

Had I not been on my knees, I would have staggered under the weight of His presence. Suddenly, nothing else mattered. I had encountered transcendence, and a gentler love than I had ever imagined. I remember thinking, *Lord, do anything You want to me, anything, just don't ever go away from me! Don't ever let me be without this sense of Your presence!*

I love how Piper expressed this experience:

> There are no words
> To speak the substance of my soul
> And joy to God, nor yet extol
> His worth above the vast rebirth
> Of all my dreams. No dancing mirth
> Can suit or satisfy the kind
> Of tearful pleasure that I find
> When I recall what I have lost
> By his decree, and what it cost
> To see my God.[16]

To see God, to know Him—the pleasure is worth the cost, even when it is paid for with tears.

All the other attributes of God resonate from His transcendence. If He is truly good, then His goodness transcends any thought or measurement our human minds can conjure. If He is faithful, and kind and compassionate, and just and merciful, and loving and patient and generous, He is all those things to a degree that surpasses anything we can imagine.

Paul wrote to the Romans, "Oh, the depth of the riches both of the wisdom and knowledge of God! How unsearchable are His judgments and unfathomable His ways!" (11:33 NASB).

In yet another passage, the apostle fumbled for words as he wrote, "Thanks be to God for His indescribable gift" (2 Corinthians 9:15 NASB).

Every gesture, every contact God initiates with us comes from His transcendent nature. Sometimes we will understand; sometimes we won't.

The psalmist wrote, "Your way was in the sea, and Your paths in the mighty waters, and Your footprints may not be known." Mysterious, unfathomable, God's doings are beyond knowing. Yet, in the next verse he tells us, "You led Your people like a flock by the hand of Moses and Aaron" (77:19, 20 NASB).

A callused hand grips a shepherd's rod; nail-scarred, sandaled feet leave prints on a gritty desert floor, and God leads in paths that cannot be mistaken.

Transcendent, beyond our ability to comprehend, but still knowable, trackable into unexpected territories of delight.

Revealing Himself

God still speaks to us in our catastrophes. When we are ready to listen, when our asking "why" finally yields to the more important "who," God speaks. And God tells us what we *must* understand if we are going to retain sanity and achieve any sense of serenity in the midst of our disasters: *I am all that you need; more than that, I am everything you think you want, everything your heart craves, and everything you never knew you wanted.*

I must understand this about God: He isn't like me, and He isn't like you either. He will cause things to happen that we don't like and don't understand. His purposes will not often be clear, although we can always be sure of one thing: In whatever catastrophe we find ourselves, God is there too, and He wants to reveal Himself to us, and to bring us into deeper levels of intimacy with Him.

When the psalmist spoke of the mysterious, transcendent nature of God, God walking on the seas and leaving no footprints, I doubt that he considered it a prophecy. But centuries later, God in flesh would walk across storm-churned seas. Jesus would step onto the foam stirred by buffeting waves, and His disciples, seeing Him in the distance, would be terrified by the unexplainable. Yet, days later, Jesus would describe Himself in common, understandable terms: the Shepherd of Israel.

This is God presented with no apologies, no excuses. Sometimes understood. Sometimes mysterious and confusing, terrifying.

But always, always, He surpasses our imagination. He is beyond our ability to fully understand. Always, He ultimately exceeds our hopes and dreams.

It Still Hurts

We cling to Paul's words in Romans 8:28: "And we know that in all things God works for the good of those who love him, who have been called according to his purpose."

This verse convinces us that there is a grand plan.

There are noble purposes that we can only see with the eyes of faith. What is happening to us is fitting into that plan for our good, for our best, for the glory of the kingdom of God.

Dallas Willard said it this way:

> All is well, even in the midst of specific suffering and
> loss. . . . For we are always looking at the larger scene
> in which love rules: Where all things, (no matter
> what) work together for good to those who love God
> and are drawn into his purposeful actions on earth.[17]

But, still, it hurts.

Job, in agony, says, "God can do anything to me, even kill me, but I'll still hope in him."[18] Turn a page and hear him cry out, "Nothing helps! No matter what I do, it still hurts."

This is often the reality we live with. My sister Susie sat and wept by her daughter Erin's bedside in intensive care after surgery to remove a tumor entangled in Erin's spinal canal. "I trust God," Susan said, "but my heart is breaking."

She said it again after the second surgery, and after the third, the fourth, and the fifth. Today, she watches her beloved daughter, a mother of three, struggle against pain and paralysis to do the simplest, most mundane mothering tasks.

A friend calls me, weeping at the news of her daughter's crumbling marriage. "It hurts so bad. I trust God, but sometimes the pain is unbearable."

Our lives flesh out the truth of Brennan Manning's words:

> We presume . . . that trust will ease confusion, dull
> the pain, redeem the times. The cloud of witnesses in

> Hebrews 11 testifies that it is not so. Our trust does
> not bring final clarity on this earth. It does not still
> the chaos or dull the pain or provide a crutch. When
> all else is unclear, the heart of trust says "Into Your
> hands I commend my spirit."[19]

This is what the theology of transcendence asks of us: to release ourselves to God, in spite of our pain, while writhing in it, because we know, in the depths of our beings, that there is truly a "larger scene where love rules."

This is our consolation. "The soul, with its living faith in God, always sees him acting behind happenings which bewilder our senses."[20]

Behind Heaven's Drape

But sometimes, on that rare occasion, God will pull back heaven's drape and let us peek behind those "bewildering happenings," and the glory of it stirs our souls to worship.

It happened like that for the mission team to the Amazon jungle, and for Jim and Carolyn, and for all of us who knew about his accident, for all of us who wondered what God was up to.

In the holy, unfathomable way of God, He prompted one of the team members to contact a doctor in the Brazilian town where Jim was treated before he was flown home. He was a well-schooled surgeon, a learned man, but he was not a Christian. Would he be interested in replacing an American surgeon to treat jungle villagers aboard a hospital ship on the Amazon River?

The doctor was willing, but he wanted to be sure the entire team understood: "I don't believe in your invisible God."

He would practice medicine among them, but he would not participate in their Christian ministry.

For the next week, the doctor worked alongside the missionaries, listening as they shared the gospel, watching them pray and study together, watching them serve tirelessly, lovingly, in the name of Christ. He thought often of the American surgeon who had been willing to leave "the other world," as he thought of it, and give his time in the jungle. At the end of the trip, he was deeply moved. In tears, he said, "I will think about your invisible God."

A few days later, after he had returned home, he visited a tiny, native evangelical church and walked down the aisle when the invitation was given to trust Jesus.

It was not a decision made lightly. In the region where he lives, witchcraft is prevalent, spiritual oppression intense. Yet he dared to commit to Christ, publicly. He dared to join a Bible study and begin the journey of faith in the company of other believers. He dared to believe in the invisible God.

Who could have envisioned the eternal outcome of a terrifying fall, a grueling journey of pain, and a distraught and despairing group of Christian servants huddled together in prayer on the deck of a ship on the Amazon River?

Only God.

Because His thoughts are not our thoughts; His ways are not our ways.

Transcendence Descending

A family counselor told the story of trying to work with a young man whose face had been disfigured in an accident. He carried himself as though ashamed, his head down so the hair he'd grown long would always cover his scars. During therapy, he sat slumped, his face angled toward the floor, never looking up, always hiding behind the curtain of hair. The therapist tried every ploy to get the young man to look at her.

One day, as the session got under way, the therapist left her chair and settled herself quietly on the floor in front of her patient's chair and looked up into the young man's tortured face. The breakthrough was instantaneous. As eyes met, trust erupted, and a new kind of dynamic filled the room.

When I heard this story, I thought of the psalmist's words, "You stoop down to make me great" (18:35).

God, so far above us, reigning in majesty and beauty that would consume us with its intensity, communes with us in the only way Transcendence can: by stooping down. Making Himself lower than the angels, He takes His place among us, and then, wonder of wonders, drops onto the floor in front of us and washes our feet so that we can be whole. So that we can be "great."

Our pains and sufferings are the stuff of our lives. Pascal wrote that "man is dependent and always liable to be exposed to a thousand and one accidents that inevitably will cause distress."[21] There is no escaping this truth: We are scarred and injured, and will be more scarred and injured before we breathe our last. But God, who is transcendent, wants to make Himself known to us, and how else, but by stooping down, entering into our chaos with us?

Can there be a more extravagant display of love and gentleness than that the highest King of Glory should come down from His throne in order to peer up into our downcast faces, so that we might see the scars on His?

The catastrophe of Calvary has no meaning without the theology of transcendence.

His presence in our lives has no ultimate significance apart from His transcendence.

Unless He is higher than the heavens, beyond our comprehending, He offers me nothing more than I can give myself, nothing more than I can beg from you.

The theology of transcendence assures us that, in spite of our losses, all is well. Love is ruling our lives—the unfathomable love of God, poured out for us at Calvary. It is a love that exceeds all measuring, expressed in kindness that has no limits.

Faith enables us to partake of that love and bask in that kindness, for "faith sees the reality of the unseen or invisible, and it includes a readiness to act as if the good anticipated were already in hand because of the reality of God."[22]

The reality of God is first and foremost this: that He is more wildly in love with us than we can ever imagine; that His plans for us to live in joyous fellowship with Him and to share His kingdom override all our smaller plans, all our puny desires. Nothing we can conjure up, in terms of entertainment, luxury, and good times can compare with all that He wants us to enjoy in His presence throughout eternity.

Henri Nouwen wrote, "We are called to see the world as God sees it; that is what theology is all about."[23]

The theology of transcendence compels us to see the world as bigger, more romantic, more astoundingly mysterious than our minds can contain, and its Maker as the One who can satisfy us and fill us with peace that passes all understanding.

 TRACKING GRACE

WE WOULD VERY SOON BECOME CONTEMPTUOUS OF A
GOD WHOM WE COULD FIGURE OUT LIKE A PUZZLE OR
LEARN TO USE LIKE A TOOL. NO, IF GOD IS WORTH OUR
ATTENTION AT ALL, HE MUST BE A GOD WE CAN LOOK UP
TO—A GOD WE MUST LOOK UP TO.[24]

—EUGENE PETERSON

Do you not know? Have you not heard?
The LORD is the everlasting God,
the Creator of the ends of the earth.
He will not grow tired or weary,
and his understanding no one can fathom.

—ISAIAH 40:28

1. What perplexing situation have you faced re-
    cently?

2. What does it mean to you to think in terms of a
    "larger story where love rules"?

3. Read Philippians 3:20–21 and Ephesians 2:1–10. Write a paragraph (or two) summarizing that "larger story." How do you see your circumstances fitting into that larger picture?

4. Read Psalm 123. Write your own prayer based on verses 1 and 2, describing what it looks like for you to lift up your eyes, to look to the hand of your master, who is God.

OUR SOUL IS LOVED SO
PRECISELY BY HIM,
OUR HIGHEST GOOD,
THAT IT IS BEYOND ALL HUMAN
UNDERSTANDING.
IN TRUTH, NO HUMAN ALIVE
CAN FATHOM HOW MUCH,
HOW SWEETLY AND TENDERLY,
OUR MAKER LOVES US.[1]

JULIAN OF NORWICH

And I pray that you, being rooted and established
in love, may have power, together with all the
saints, to grasp how wide and long and high and
deep is the love of Christ, and to know this love
that surpasses knowledge—that you may be filled
to the measure of all the fullness of God.
                              —EPHESIANS 3:17–19

CHAPTER THREE

The Realm of the "Totally Other"

GOD IS LOVE

I was checking out the greeting cards in Wal-Mart the other day when I heard a man's singing voice coming from the next aisle. I turned the corner and saw a young daddy leaning over a baby girl strapped snugly onto a shopping cart. Not the least bit self-conscious, he was singing love songs to her in a pleasant, mellow voice. With just a hint of vibrato, his voice carried over the bustle and noise of hurried shoppers, some of whom turned to stare at him in amusement.

His baby daughter stared at him in adoration.

In that moment, an aisle in Wal-Mart became a holy place.

Had I been as *un*-self-conscious as that young father, I would have dropped to my knees to worship God. I knew with absolute certainty that He had sent me to that place, at that very moment, to remind me of Zephaniah's words,

"The LORD your God is with you. . . . He will quiet you with his love, he will rejoice over you with singing" (3:17).

During a very dark period in my life, my sister Susie wrote that verse on a card and mailed it to me. The imagery of it stunned me—God erupting in song because He loves me so much!

It was a soul-staggering realization that day.

It staggers me still today.

Quantum Leap of Faith

Grasping the truth of God's love, beyond the mere acceptance of it as a theological truth, may be the most difficult challenge we ever face.

In his book *The God Who Won't Let Go,* Peter van Breeman wrote that believing in God's love requires us to "make a quantum leap of faith. . . . to leap into the totally other realm of God's love. . . . a leap we have to make again and again. Over and over, Scripture invites us to believe the startling, wonderful, almost-too-good-to-be-true revelation: God's longing is for each of us."[2]

Frederick Buechner referred to this longing, this love, as the "unflagging lunacy of God."[3]

Unflagging lunacy, to human reasoning, because it reaches out and embraces "the unending seaminess of man."

And woman.

God's love embraces us, in our "seaminess," whether we can feel it or not.

Entirely "Other"

Nothing in our world, in the human realm, adequately equates to God's love, although we may experience what Philip Yancey calls "rumors" of it. We see a parent with a child, a lover with his bride, a friend with a friend, and a faint scent of the infinite wafts across our senses. Hints of a transcendent love tease our souls. But the final truth is this: The love of God is "entirely other."

"The mystics have always deeply experienced this truth, that God is entirely *Other*. This is especially true when we attempt to speak of God's love. The love of God differs radically, entirely, from all human love which we have ever experienced."[4] It is a "totally other realm."

Probably no place on the face of the earth is as totally other as the realm of the ocean depths.

My sister Paula called me from her hotel room just minutes after she went scuba diving for the first time. She wasn't supposed to dive because of health issues and concerns about the mix of elements and medications. But after sitting on the deck of the boat and watching her husband and friends emerge from the water with the thrill of adventure on their faces, Paula was determined. The next day, when the group put out to sea, she begged one of the master divers to take her down. She explained her medications, he thought for a minute, and then he said, "Let's go."

"I did it! Can you believe it? It's like another world!" she raved. "You feel like you're in another universe. It's so beautiful—all the creatures! Oh, there just aren't any words to describe it!"

And so she came home, took a certification course, and when the group of friends went to Cozumel a few months later, Paula took her own diving equipment and joined them in the subterranean exploration of another world.

As I've studied and meditated on the love of God, Paula's experience keeps coming to mind. Because the love of God, like the terrain beneath the waters of the ocean, is "another world." It is infinite. Because we are finite, we cannot ever fully understand it anymore than we can fully plumb the depths of the ocean and uncover all its mysteries.

Like Paula, we can dive into it and experience new depths of wonder and delight, or we can sit on the deck and yearn.

His Very Nature

This is our challenge, daily, hourly: to accept that God's love is baffling, perplexing; to believe that His love is lavish enough to be more than adequate for whatever traumas and terrors await us. If we do, we can expect to encounter rich mysteries and wonders that will startle our souls and bring us into sweet communion with God that is unlike anything we've ever known, or known we could hope for.

> God's perfection is his love. All his divine rights,
> his power, his justice, his righteousness, his mercy,
> his fatherhood—every divine attribute we think
> to ascribe to him—rests upon his love.
> God's love is what he *is*.[5]
>
> —GEORGE MACDONALD

Here's what we must grab hold of: God's nature is love. He cannot be anything other than what He is.

We can misunderstand God's love, and resist it, but we cannot alter it. We can cower from it, misjudge it, and malign it, but we cannot escape it.

We cannot change the fact that God loves us—that it is impossible for Him to *not* love us.

And being loved by God, recognizing it, reveling in it, is the most outrageous experience of all.

This is the good news of the gospel of Jesus Christ.

This is truth that makes life worth living, with all its crises and catastrophes, the large ones and the small.

I wish it hadn't taken me so long to get it.

Maybe then I would have been able to share it with Sam.

A Question of Love

Sam is one of the most brilliant young men I've ever met. A doctoral candidate in psychology, he struck up a conversation with me one day in a bookstore when he saw the stack of books I was buying. I don't think he had ever met anyone who read Pierre de Caussade. When I told him it was a book of spiritual insights from a great Christian thinker, he said, "So, you must be a Christian."

So began the first of several conversations. Sam seemed always to be in the bookstore when I was there. He seemed always to be looking to engage me in a conversation about God. He considered himself a Christian, although what he believed defies all orthodoxy. Most of his comments were intended to provoke, challenge, and rattle me, and they often did. But one question haunts me still, months after our last encounter.

"Why?" Sam asked. Over and over again, the unrelenting question punctuated every conversation.

"You're always talking about trusting Jesus, making a decision for Christ. Why? Why would anyone want to know Jesus? And don't tell me it's to escape hell, because what if I don't believe in hell?"

While I stammered and stuttered, Sam barreled on. "Last time I checked, belief in hell wasn't a 'deal-breaker' with God. You don't have to believe in hell to be a Christian, at least not according to your creed. All you have to do is believe in Jesus and accept Him as your savior, right?

So, if I'm not worried about hell, what's the benefit in knowing and trusting Christ?"

More stammering.

"And don't tell me it's because Christians enjoy a better life with Christ, because I know too many Christians who suffer through terrible illnesses and tragedies—huge messes, really—and then die. So if I'm not worrying about hell right now, what does Jesus bring to the table?"

I didn't know what to say to Sam. I left those conversations feeling frustrated and confused. I grew to dread seeing his motorcycle parked at my favorite neighborhood bookstore.

Today, I'd shout with joy if I saw Sam's bike. Because, today, I know the answer to his question.

Jesus brings *Jesus* to the table!

Love's Invasion

Jesus gives us Himself.

And with Jesus we get every treasure of heaven. As Paul told the Colossians: "For in Christ all the fullness of the Deity lives in bodily form, and you have been given fullness in Christ, who is the head over every power and authority" (2:9).

> *It's in Christ that we find out who we are and what we are living for. Long before we first heard of Christ and got our hopes up, he had his eye on us, had designs on us for glorious living, part of the overall purpose he is working out in everything and everyone.*
> —EPHESIANS 1:11–12 THE MESSAGE

Jesus is at the heart of God's love. In Jesus, love invaded this "enemy-occupied territory"; in Jesus, love declared that "the rightful king has landed!"[6]

"To all who received him, to those who believed in his name, he gave the right to become children of God" (John 1:12).

This is the big story that dwarfs all our smaller stories. This is the story "in which everything eventually comes together, a narrative in which all the puzzling parts finally fit. . . . God is telling this story, remember. It is a large, capacious story."[7]

Is it a wild tale, or is it reality?

For C. S. Lewis, it was the very wildness of it, the oddness and unexpectedness of it that made him choose to believe it.

> Reality, in fact, is usually something you could not
> have guessed. That is one of the reasons I believe
> Christianity. If it offered us just the kind of universe
> we had always expected, I should feel we were
> making it up. But in fact, it is not the sort of thing
> anyone would have made up. It has just that queer
> twist about it that real things have.[8]

I look around me and I see real sin.

I look inside myself and I see more of the same— pride, hypocrisy, a critical spirit.

I look at the testimony of saints, of the Scriptures, and I see the real love of God, not a sappy emotion but a powerful love that invades and claims. It rescues me from myself and from my sin. It romances me, woos me into intimacy with the King of Kings. It is love that declares I am the beloved child of God, adored and cherished and destined for a future glory I can't even begin to imagine.

This is what we get with Jesus.

His every gesture, every word, every movement, emanates from the divine nature that is characterized by love.

All That He Is

Not a stoic nature, dispassionate and cold, it is neither weak nor indulgent. Would I want a love that would tolerate my false self and leave me stewing in my sin-sickened state? In Christ, in His incarnation, God has "made room for wrath and love to run wild."[9] His wrath is for the sin that destroys us; His love heals and restores.

Jesus, loving us, loving the Father, stormed the temple in fury and ousted the self-serving, irreverent merchants who were taking advantage of the poor.

Enraged at the prejudice and hypocrisy of the Pharisees, Jesus called them vipers and compared their lives to fancied-up graves that house the rotting flesh of the dead.

Jesus shed tears in the garden before His death. Weeping, He looked over the people of Jerusalem, yearning to gather them close to His heart like a mother hen would shelter her chicks beneath her wings.

He rejoiced and celebrated the marriage of two lovebirds in Cana. Our Lord expressed compassion to Mary and Martha, sharing their sorrow, grieving with them when their brother, Lazarus, died.

All the love we've yearned for becomes ours through Jesus. We are unconditionally accepted, cleansed, set on a course that will lead us to heaven. And in the meantime, we have His companionship, complete with kindness, mercy, and tender care.

It is love that values us, dignifies us, and gives us purpose and meaning. It is love that gives us a share in glory so huge and so majestic that "no eye has seen, no ear has heard, no mind has conceived what God has prepared for those who love him" (1 Corinthians 2:9).

This is what we get when we get Jesus.

And not only Jesus, but we get the Father as well.

Paul wrote, "We look at this Son and see the God who cannot be seen" (Colossians 1:15 THE MESSAGE).

Brennan Manning wrote, "For the disciple, God is no other than as he is seen in the person of Jesus. . . . Clear-minded, hardheaded, and softhearted, Jesus revealed in his ministry of mercy the face of the compassionate God."[10]

Peter Kreeft said it this way: "We know what God is like. Jesus. God is infinite, eternal absolute, unqualified love. Everything He does, therefore, is love. Everything that comes to us, therefore is His kiss."[11]

God's kiss was Jesus' touch when He reached out and put His hands on the diseased skin of the leper.

God's kiss was Jesus wrapping His arms around children, blessing them, welcoming them. God's kiss was Jesus having supper with the lowlifes, the street people, the shunned ones hovering beyond the fringes of society, maligned and rejected by religious folks with warped ideas about God.

It was Jesus who loved the underdog, who fought for the abused, who reached out to the untouchables.

Jesus, lifting up the woman thrown into the dirt at His feet, showed us the heart of His Father; Jesus, feeding a hungry mob; Jesus, sharing his life with a motley crew of Hebrews who smelled of fish and sweat—this is God! He is not deterred by our stench, or our selfishness, or our sin. He is not surprised when we fail. He is not disgusted with our weakness.

In Jesus, the invisible Father is presented in a physical, emotional, and spiritual context we can relate to, and we see the Friend of sinners, who for love "gave his one and only Son that whoever believe in him shall not perish but have eternal life" (John 3:16).

You can't get Jesus without getting all that God the

Father offers—and all that He is, all that He wants you to have, and all that infinite love can design.

And you can't get Jesus without getting the indwelling of the Holy Spirit.

Jesus, on the eve of His death, told the disciples:

I will ask the Father, and he will give you another Counselor to be with you forever—the Spirit of truth. The world cannot accept him, because it neither sees him nor knows him. But you know him, for he lives with you and will be in you. I will not leave you as orphans; I will come to you. Before long, the world will not see me anymore, but you will see me. Because I live, you also will live. On that day you will realize that I am in my Father, and you are in me, and I am in you.

—JOHN 14:16–20

Knowing Our Adopter

Is there a sadder, more desolate word than *orphan?* Is there any word that better describes a life without His presence?

Jesus once asked His disciples, "Are you going to abandon me?" And Peter answered, for all of us, "Lord, to whom would we run?" (See John 6:67–68.)

We sing, "Jesus loves me, this I know." The lilting melody sweetens our souls. The truth of the message should stagger us—this wild and odd and unexpected tale of love, love made personal and knowable. Love that, "by blossoming into other notions of passion, wrath, and eagerness . . . widens our notion of God."[12]

Is there anything we need more than to have our notion of God widened? How our churches would be changed if we could grasp the deep, deep love of God and find release from bondage to the law, from bondage to our "programs," to find ourselves set free from the painful bindings of our self-expectations and perfectionism. How our unbelieving friends and family would be blessed if we, God's people, could learn to live in the truths of His love and express to others the exuberant nature of a compassionate God who is eager to commune with us, a God who loves us with a kind of gut-wrenching emotion that drove Him to Calvary's cross!

How I need to know and understand the love of God for me, in all its wildness, so that I can say with the apostle Paul that any loss, any suffering, is nothing more than "rubbish" compared to the "surpassing greatness of knowing Christ Jesus my Lord" (Philippians 3:8).

The saints throughout history have echoed his words to the Corinthians: "Though outwardly we are wasting away, yet inwardly we are being renewed day by day. For our light and momentary troubles are achieving for us an eternal glory that far outweighs them all" (2 Corinthians 4:16–17).

That glory is *knowing Jesus*.

It outweighs everything, Paul said. "I want to *know* Christ and the power of his resurrection and the fellowship of sharing in his sufferings," because knowing Jesus—the incarnate God whose very nature is love—surpasses everything (Philippians 3:10, italics added).

It surpasses comfortable living conditions, a full bank account, a clean bill of health, obedient kids, a loving spouse, a satisfying career. It surpasses all that we might aspire to, more than the American dream offers.

Paul said that, for the Christian, troubles in this life achieve something: knowledge of Christ. He was saying, "Whatever it takes to know Christ better, that's what I want to experience. If sharing His sufferings will make that happen, then bring them on!"

To the Depths

This isn't a typical response when catastrophe strikes, is it?

When pain stings, our thoughts spin helter-skelter. And the first question that erupts is not, how much of Jesus' love can my heart contain before it bursts? No, if you're like me and most of the people I know, the first question is this: How can a God who says He loves me allow this terrible thing?

Whether it's a large or small mess we must deal with on any given day, we insist on defining what we think God's love should look like. We insist on prescribing how a loving God should deal with us—what He should and shouldn't do.

I remember the day my sister Susie called with a diagnosis of cancer. Anger boiled up inside me, and I wanted to run into the street and scream, "This stinks, God! Do You call this love?"

While Ken's father lay in the hospital for three months following cancer surgery before dying an excruciating death, I often questioned, "Lord, is this any way to treat Your faithful servant?"

At times, during Ken's mother's recent fight against ovarian cancer, a fight that ended in an agonizing death, I wondered how God could let her suffer so terribly.

We ridicule the pedantic "love means never having to say I'm sorry," but our hearts come up with an equally foolish mantra: "Love means never having to say *I'm suffering*."

Because we fail to grasp that God's love is "totally other."

It is love that operates from a unique agenda, *very* unlike our own—one Larry Crabb labeled the "Emanuel Agenda."

> The [Emanuel] Agenda is on track. . . . Our highest
> calling, our deepest joy, is to celebrate His availability
> by drawing near to Him, not to use Him to make our
> lives better, but to enjoy Him for who He is.[13]

John Piper wrote that "this is God's universal purpose for all Christian suffering: more contentment in God and less satisfaction in self and the world. . . . Strong saints say, 'Every significant advance I have ever made in grasping the depths of God's love and growing deep with Him has come through suffering.'"[14]

Faith calls me to embrace this truth, to understand that "sometimes His kiss is full of tears."[15]

My flesh resists it mightily.

The Point of Amazement

Few Christians have written as passionately about God's love as Teresa of Avila, a sixteenth-century Spanish saint. Fewer still have written so honestly about their pain.

There is agony that "breaks and grinds the soul to pieces," and yet in her writings she included this:

> What a tremendous good it is to suffer trials and
> persecutions for Him. For the increase of the love of
> God I saw in my soul and many other things reached
> such a point that I was amazed; and this makes me
> unable to stop desiring trials. . . . Give me trials,
> Lord, give me persecutions.[16]

Asking God for trials is not on my daily prayer list, but I do have to admit that every life-changing, mind-altering truth I've ever learned about God's love for me has come packaged in pain. My experiences are pallid compared to what others have suffered, but when pain has struck, God has been there for me. His love has amazed me.

I can't explain it. It's just true, and not for me alone.

"Consider that He is altogether lovely; He is made up of love, goodness and all excellencies. . . . Ask of them that by faith have seen Him."[17]

A friend whose husband left her after a long marriage has seen Him. Her testimony: "I'm aware of the love of God in ways I never was before."

My friend John, who has Lou Gehrig's disease, has seen Him. "Never have I been so conscious of Jesus' love; never have I been so in love with my Lord. Never have I been so full of joy." His wife, Margaret, echoes his words.

Gerald Sittser, in his book *A Grace Disguised*, wrote about "How the Soul Grows Through Loss." Telling the story of the deaths of his wife, daughter, and mother-in-law in a car crash, he brings the reader alongside him as he travels the path of grief, dealing with his pain and confusion thoughtfully, honestly, and humbly. While he admits that he is "still bewildered" by the loss, acknowledging that he will "bear the mark of the tragedy" the rest of his life, he also wrote, "My soul has grown because it has been awakened to the goodness and love of God. . . . My life is being transformed. Though I have endured pain, I believe that the outcome is going to be wonderful."[18]

In the final pages, he wrote that he has been enlarged by his loss, that his "capacity to live life well and know God intimately" has increased.

The stories of suffering saints who wouldn't exchange their pain for less of God would fill more books than I would have time to write in a dozen lifetimes. The accounts would differ only in the names and circumstances; the theme would always be the same: that God's love for

us is "not abstract but deeply personal; not a general prin-
ciple, but a bold, creative affection for each of us as we are
(and not as we feel we should be)."[19]

Being loved like this—"as we are"—is what every human heart yearns for. For most of us, suffering is the experience that opens us up to welcome that love in portions
we never imagined we could contain. At pain's prompting,
we look to Jesus and see love through eyes that, until
washed by tears, were blurred by the decaying bounty of
this temporal life. And we are amazed.

Love Opposed

It's important to be reminded that we have an Enemy
whose most urgent mission is to delude us about the nature
of God's deep love for us.

My friend John reminded me of that one recent Sunday morning when we met in the church foyer over a cup
of coffee. (It's always fascinating and humbling to hear his
views in the context of his struggle with Lou Gehrig's
disease.)

"Jan, understanding God's love for us is the most
transforming thing that can happen to us! His love meets
our every desire, our every longing. He heals us from the
inside out." He paused, shook his head. "You can't imagine how many men I talk to who just can't believe that
God loves them," he said.

"It's not just men," I said. I was thinking of my own
struggle to come to terms with God's love for me, and
thinking of the many women I've known who share that
same struggle.

"We forget that there's active warfare going on, Jan.
Satan doesn't want us to believe that God loves us. He'll
do anything to keep us from believing it."

I needed that reminder. We all do.

And never more so than when we are in pain.

If Satan can convince us that a loving God wouldn't let awful things happen to us, he has scored a victory.

If he can keep us asking how a loving God could let us, or our loved ones, suffer, if he can keep us bowed under the weight of that question, feeling forsaken and frightened, then the cause of hell will have been served. God will have been maligned. And Satan will be thrilled.

Satan loves it when he can keep us imagining a God who takes pleasure in seeing His creatures squirm.

That's our problem.

Influenced by the Enemy, we begin to "imagine" God. We forget the truth about Him, about His character, about the nature of His love for us and the "kind intention of His will" (Ephesians 1:5 NASB).

We shrink back from the only true source of comfort and nurse our pain in bitterness and fear. And Satan's minions celebrate. Can't you just see it? If you can't, try reading C. S. Lewis's *Screwtape Letters*.

Screwtape, the senior demon, "Abysmal Sublimity Undersecretary," explains to his nephew Wormwood, a novice tempter, that the demons and all the causes of hell suffer a major loss "if a Christian consciously directs his prayers 'Not to what I think Thou art but to what Thou knowest Thyself to be.'"[20]

Put more simply, here are Screwtape's instructions: Keep Christians as far away as possible from the truth about *what God knows to be true about Himself*. Keep them always trying to shape God into a form of their own making, based on anything but the truth, and you'll be serving well the Underkingdom.

Spiritual warfare is a reality for every Christian. We must fight against anything and anyone that would attempt to malign the love of God. It will not be easy, but our safety lies in the armor of God. The first piece is the belt of truth. Everything else hangs on that.

A Grieved Heart

What about those times when we lose the battle?

What about those times when, in our pain and grief, we rant and rail against God? Those times when we lose sight of the truth and fall into despair?

Haven't we all, in moments of great pain, cried out against God? Haven't we all doubted His love and accused Him of crimes against us?

I remember a night when I was so angry and confused about my life and my family that I blurted out, "I hate you, God!"

Horror washed over me.

What had I done?

Terrified and repentant, I dropped to my knees and begged God's forgiveness. For days, weeks, I fought a lonely battle with despair. (How could I share with anyone that I'm so wicked that I would tell God I hated Him?) I grabbed hold of every verse I could find that addressed forgiveness, reading them with relief mixed with guilt and uncertainty, gaining a fragile peace.

With time, the event was forgotten, buried under grace upon grace, until recently, when a thoughtful writer (I don't remember who) recounted a similar experience of a Christian shrieking at God in fury. The author, a counselor, had responded calmly to the account of the outburst, comparing it to a toddler's tantrum.

As I read the story, all the horror of that night swept over me again, but just as quickly came the realization that God had seen me for the distraught child that I was. And almost smiling, I looked up at God and saw Him as the Father that He is.

I let my imagination capture the image, seeing myself as I had seen my own children as toddlers, knowing their storm of anger would pass, knowing that nothing they said in the heat of frustration would alter the fact that they are *mine*. Nothing they could say or do would stop me from loving them.

I think Asaph might have been writing about just such an experience in Psalm 73:21–24:

> *When my heart was grieved and my spirit embittered,*
> *I was senseless and ignorant; I was a brute beast before you.*
> *Yet I am always with you;*
> *You hold me by my right hand.*
> *You guide me with your counsel,*
> *and afterward you will take me into glory.*

Asaph had experienced a "sour" heart. That's a more literal rendering of what we've translated "grieved and embittered." It's more graphic, isn't it? Much like our stomachs sour when we eat unhealthy, unwholesome foods, our hearts can sour when we load up on falsehoods about God; and out of a sour heart comes senseless, stupid behavior.

We act like brute beasts before God (or toddlers throwing temper tantrums).

Yet—ah, what a beautiful word that is!—*yet*, or *even though*, I'm foolish, brutish, ignorant, and acting out of a sour heart, God is with me. He hasn't abandoned me.

Not only is He with me, He *touches* me—unlike human love that withdraws from us when we're brutes. "His grip stronger than a lion's paw."[21] He holds me tight, unlike conditional love that wants to distance itself from ignorant fools.

Here's the beautiful picture of that Psalm: God hangs on to me, even when all human reason says He should let go and turn away from me in disgust. Paul was saying much the same thing when he wrote that nothing can separate us from the love of God in Christ Jesus.

> *I'm absolutely convinced that nothing—*
> *nothing living or dead, angelic or demonic, today or tomorrow,*
> *high or low, thinkable or unthinkable—*
> *absolutely nothing can get between us and God's love*
> *because of the way that Jesus our Master has embraced us.*
> —ROMANS 8:38–39 THE MESSAGE

Nothing is stronger than God's love for you—nothing difficult; nothing cruel and harsh, nothing dangerous and painful—nothing! Nothing can interfere, or interrupt the deep, powerful flow of His love toward you.

Like the ocean, His love is immeasurable, unstoppable. It cannot be contained, or curtailed, or controlled, or contaminated—even when we've sinned in ugly, despicable, immature ways. Even when, in our pain, we have lashed out and bitterly denounced His love.

Amazing thought, isn't it? After I've acted like a fool, felt bitterness and fury toward God, and behaved like a savage, God still loves me. He is still with me.

God is still intent on sharing His glory with me, and nothing is going to keep that from happening—so wild and unexpected is His love for you and me, so strong is the grip of the Lion of Judah.

Heaven's Music

For years, neuroscientists have been curious about the effects of music on the human brain. Using advanced brain imaging, researchers tell us that the rostromedial pre-frontal cortex, which processes emotion, also tracks music. They report that the brain's right hemisphere processes rhythm, while the left processes melody. The whole brain, not just a small cluster of cells, is engaged in receiving and responding to music.

Researchers were filled with excitement when recent experiments proved that music has the ability to ease physical pain and relieve anxiety and distress.

This, of course, comes as no surprise to the innumerable saints down through the centuries who have long been aware of the power of heaven's music.

The Creator of song who designed the brain knitted its cells together and set into motion the neurons to fit us with a complex, amazing organ that would be receptive, in its totality, to the joy of His love.

Oh, how I wish I had come to understand the truth about His love earlier in my walk of faith.

For far too long I lived in fear of breaking a "rule," fear of appearing less than perfect, less than adequate or proficient in the eyes of people close to me. I was preoccupied with preventing disasters, coping feebly with the ones I couldn't prevent, and trying to define the walk of faith in terms of behavior, or blessings. To me, blessings would include things such as a strong body, financial prosperity, book contracts, and healthy family dynamics. When things went wrong, as they inevitably did, the first thing I wondered about was God's love.

But as seasons of suffering came and went, I discovered that other "comforts" failed to ease my pain or give it meaning. Nothing I studied, apart from the Word of God and the message of a loving God, offered solace or significance. I found myself haunted by the mysterious music of His love.

Almost against my will, I began to respond to that music. I was waiting, at times desperate, for the sweetness of the melody, anxious for the rhythm of grace.

Daily, I find I must make adjustments to this music of unconditional love. (I'm a recovering legalist, and I'll always struggle with that.) Heaven's melody is always heard in a key that clashes with the noise of my culture, its rhythms at odds with the tempo of my own sin nature. Daily I pray for grace to live in the reality of the truth that God's love for me isn't tied to my performance.

Often, when I am weary from the effort to dislodge old thought patterns, the sweet harmonies of the Trinity penetrate and soothe. I'm confronted with the picture of a singing God!

It is too much. God *enjoys* me! Loving me gives Him pleasure!

"The depth of His affection is such that mere words prove paltry and inadequate. So profoundly intimate is God's devotion to you that He bursts forth into sacred song."[22]

This mind-boggling love for you, and for me, moves the infinite God to music. His voice echoes off the columns that support the galaxies as He sings over the children He adores.

It is music that knows no boundaries. It can penetrate a jail cell, a hospital room, a funeral home, a classroom, and any other place you can think of. It can be heard under any circumstances, at any time, in any place.

If you're listening, you may even hear it in the aisle of a Wal-Mart.

 TRACKING GRACE

THOU WHO HAST FIRST LOVED US, O GOD, ALAS!
WE SPEAK OF IT IN TERMS OF HISTORY AS IF THOU HAST
ONLY LOVED US FIRST BUT A SINGLE TIME, RATHER THAN
THAT WITHOUT CEASING THOU HAST LOVED US FIRST
MANY TIMES AND EVERYDAY AND OUR WHOLE LIFE
THROUGH. . . . AND YET WE ALWAYS SPEAK UNGRATE-
FULLY AS IF THOU HAS LOVED US FIRST ONLY ONCE.[23]

—SOREN KIERKEGAARD

*This is how God showed his love among us: He sent his one
and only Son into the world that we might live through him.
This is love: not that we loved God, but that he loved us and
sent his Son as an atoning sacrifice for our sins.*

—1 JOHN 4:9–10

1. What is your response to the kind of love de-
    scribed above?

2. Can you relate to the idea of God's love being
    "totally other"?

3. Try imagining what it would feel like to be able to make that "quantum leap" into the unfathomable love of God. Write a paragraph describing what that experience might be like for you.

4. List some of the changes you might see in your life if you were willing to make that leap of faith into the depths of God's love.

5. David wrote, "O my Strength, I watch for you; you, O God, are my fortress, my loving God" (Psalm 59:9). Resolve to watch for God, to listen for His song, and record how His love comes through for you.

THERE'S MORE TO KNOWING
GOD THAN WE DARE IMAGINE.
IT'S TIME TO PUT ASIDE OUR
CYNICISM AND COME TO GOD,
WAITING CONSCIOUSLY,
DELIBERATELY, AND WITH
DISCIPLINE FOR THE SPIRIT TO
DELIGHT OUR SOULS WITH
THE RICH FARE OF GOD.[1]

LARRY CRABB

The LORD is good to those whose hope is in him,
to the one who seeks him.

—LAMENTATIONS 3:25

CHAPTER FOUR

The Basis for Everything

GOD IS GOOD

I once heard about a man whose daughter was stricken with breast cancer. He grieved and prayed, begging God to spare her life, offering God his life in exchange. When the old man discovered he had colon cancer, he thought, "Aha! It worked! God is going to take my life and spare my daughter's." He prepared himself to die on the operating table. When he awakened after surgery and realized that he was still alive, he was enraged.

In the days and weeks that followed, as it became obvious that he was going to recover, his family was baffled by the deep depression that settled upon him. Finally, the father explained to his daughter, "We had a deal, God and I. I was supposed to die so you could live." God had reneged, he thought. The "deal" fell through. The father waited for his daughter to die. It never occurred to the old man that both he and his daughter would live, that God would be so *good* as to heal them both.

You may be able to tell a similar story about when God changed your perception of Him. All of us, at some time, to varying degrees, doubt that God is really as good as others say He is. Or as good as we would love to believe He is. But the truth is, *He is!*

God is as good as we would like to believe He is.

God is as good as—He is *better* than—we could ever imagine Him being.

Our problem lies in our understanding of what divine goodness looks like.

What Is Good?

I use the same adjective to praise the majestic King of Kings that I use to affirm my sixty-pound Airedale when she climbs off the sofa, "Good girl, Cash."

My daughter, Molly, tries a new spice in the Thanksgiving pumpkin cobbler, and I pronounce it good.

I see a movie over the holidays and tell my friends it's good.

I use a simple multipurpose word that cannot compare to the fullness of meaning the psalmists had in mind when they wrote, "Your name is good" (52:9).

> *Taste and see that the LORD is good.*
> —PSALM 34:8

> *You are good, and what you do is good.*
> —PSALM 119:68

> *For the LORD is good and his love endures forever.*
> —PSALM 100:5

The LORD is good to all; he has compassion on all he has made.
—PSALM 145:9

What we translate "good" is a small Hebrew word with huge meaning: pleasant, beautiful, excellent, lovely, delightful, joyful, fruitful, precious, cheerful, kind, correct, virtuous, happy, right.

The definition isn't complete without a reference to the sensory context of goodness—it includes *feelings* that we associate with the most pleasant of experiences; it includes taste, touch, smell.

In our language we read "good" and think an abstract kind of "okayness," a niceness that is vague and maybe even a little anemic. And we miss the unfathomable depths of the greatness of God's heart. Eugene Peterson wrote:

> There is plenitude in God. That great fact must never
> be lost or obscured. We must not exchange this
> immense graciousness for a few scraps of human
> morality or a few shopworn proverbs. God is a vast
> reservoir of blessing who supplies us abundantly.
> If we lose touch with the reality of God,
> we will live clumsily and badly.[2]

Finding Loveliness

I confess: The times I live most badly, and clumsily, are those times when I am so consumed with my discomfort, or disaster, that I have lost touch with the reality of God's infinite, immeasurable goodness.

I wallow in guilt and self-hatred over past and present sin.

I live with low-level anxiety.

I mourn and grieve over missed opportunities.

I dread future catastrophes.

All this I do because I have lost touch with the reality of grace that could be my peace, my comfort, and my joy. I have taken refuge in the small, momentary relief I can get from an emotional outburst or in the solace of a temporary distraction.

And I am missing out on an experience with transcendent goodness.

I am missing out on an extraordinary grace.

"If God is the Supreme Good, then our highest blessedness on earth must lie in knowing Him as perfectly as possible," wrote Tozer.[3]

But of course, because we are imperfect, our knowledge of God will be imperfect. Or as one poet put it:

> 'Tis because I am mean,
> Thy ways so oft look mean to me.[4]

No credit is given for this obscure quote, buried in tiny print in Oswald Chambers' *My Utmost For His Highest*. Any one of us could have said it. In today's vernacular, it would read like this: We don't expect God to be good because we aren't good.

Chambers said it this way: "The revelation of God to me is determined by the state of my character toward God."[5]

Paul, in his letter to Titus, wrote, "To the pure, all things are pure, but to those who are corrupted and do not believe, nothing is pure" (1:15).

It all has to do with the condition of our heart; it has to do with how we view God. It all has to do with whether or not we believe His heart is filled with infinite, immeasurable goodness.

Jesus talked about this in the parable about the wealthy man who, on the eve of a long journey, entrusted his possessions to three slaves. He assigned a specific amount of money to each slave, giving to each man "according to his ability" (Matthew 25:15).

I used to give this parable mixed reviews. I've never been able to muster much excitement for the math of investing and compound interest, but I have always been intrigued by relationship dynamics, and I've come to see that this story is not so much about savings accounts and stocks and dividends. It is about how one man could be so wrong about another—and at what cost.

The master knows his people. He knows what they are capable of. Because he is a good man, he gives to all three of his slaves, even the one who is not deserving. When the master returns from his journey, he finds that two of his slaves have fulfilled their responsibilities, have honored their master by adding to his wealth. But the third, the one who was given the least, has hidden the portion entrusted to him. He has no increase for his master.

Listen to his excuse: "I was afraid I'd blow it."

Listen to his accusations: "I knew you were a harsh master, a thief, taking whatever you want, whether it's yours or not, wielding your power like a scythe, regardless of whom you hurt in the process. Who wouldn't be afraid to transact business on your behalf? I didn't want the risk."

Here is the fascinating part of this parable. This man's great wrong was not that he failed as a financial wizard. It was this: He was wrong about his master.

Translate the parable into spiritual terms and we see the story of an individual who judged God's character and found Him wanting; an individual who expected God to be harsh. "I knew that you are a hard man . . . so I was afraid" (Matthew 25:24–25).

I am embarrassed at how often I'm wrong about God.

It's easy, while writhing in pain, whether emotional or physical, to cry out, "God, you're too harsh!"

"You don't love me!"

"If you were really good, you would (do such and such a thing)."

I'm not alone in this, am I? We've all accused God of being less than good when our circumstances appear bad.

Karen Mains wrote:

> We see what we choose to look for. If you hunt for the decadent, the negative, the ugly, that is what you will see. If you search for the beautiful, the holy, the true, your eye will become practiced at finding God's loveliness everywhere.[6]

How do you practice finding God's loveliness when you live in a culture that applauds sin and mocks truth? How do you keep God's goodness in view and not become distracted and discouraged by the ugliness and evil of this sin-damaged planet?

I see it as rehearsing the truth of God's goodness until it is so deeply planted in my psyche that I can lift my eyes to the horizon, and regardless of what I see there, with the eyes of faith I see also His goodness, His amazing grace.

Often I've written this phrase from Psalms on a 4″ x 6″ card and carried it with me: "You are good, and what you do is good" (119:68). Sometimes I have to say it out loud to make my heart hear the words over the roar of the Enemy's message that is constantly slandering God's character.

The prophet Jeremiah said, "Give thanks to the Lord of hosts, For the Lord is good, for His lovingkindness is everlasting" (33:11 NASB).

The Puritan preacher Stephen Charnock wrote, "God alone is infinitely good . . . not only good, but best; not only good, but goodness itself, the supreme unconceivable goodness."[7]

If we look for His goodness against the backdrop of our suffering, we will see it, bright against the darkness, glistening with gentleness, mercy, and compassion. But "the moment we permit evil to control our imaginations, dictate the way we think, and shape our responses, we at the same time become incapable of seeing the good, the true and the beautiful."[8]

When the Unimaginable Occurs

Every believer who has chosen to accept the truth of God's goodness in the midst of catastrophe can testify to this: His goodness is an almost tangible presence in the face of pain and loss.

It is a mysterious thing, this all-encompassing blanket of goodness that God wraps us in, but it is an undisputed fact, attested to by scores of Christians who have drawn comfort from the goodness of God during bad situations. The experience is unarguable. Even when the unimaginable occurs.

As I was writing this chapter, news came of a despicable, destructive event in the lives of some people I know. A child I know and love was the victim of someone's cruel perversion. Suddenly evil seemed the greater truth; "goodness" seemed foreign and distant. I was desperate to grab hold of God's goodness.

Digging into familiar Scriptures, looking back at the "tracks of grace" from years past, I couldn't escape the truth of God's goodness. Over and over I saw reminders of His kindness and His mercy. Over and over I found accounts of how He healed and restored and helped and sustained. I couldn't mistake the markers of His goodness.

Frederick Buechner wrote about the safety and sanctity

of "having-beenness." His "having been there" for me is "inviolate. . . . In all the vast and empty reaches of the universe it can never be otherwise."[9]

All that God has done for me in the past will stand— markers that no one can ever tear down, pointing me into the arms of God who is ready at all times to be all that I need, in all circumstances.

Because of the certainty of His Word and the evidence of His "having-beenness," I know that God can and will accomplish His best, even in the worst circumstances.

Joseph, remembering the cruelty of his brothers and the years of prison and suffering brought on by their actions, told them, "You intended to harm me, but God intended it for good to accomplish what is now being done, the saving of many lives" (Genesis 50:20).

Thomas More wrote that "the brethren of Joseph could never have done him so much good with their love and favour as they did him with their malice and hatred."[10]

But who would have imagined it?

Who would have imagined the glorious, life-giving outcome when the unimaginable happened in Joseph's life?

Maybe this is our greatest challenge: to refuse to try to figure out *how* God is going to do it; to refuse to look at the obstacles and the impossibilities; to remember that with God all things are possible.

Even when the unimaginable occurs.

Surprising Comfort

In many instances, God has been known to dazzle suffering saints with His goodness.

My sister Susie has endured cancer, job crises, and personal disappointments, but nothing has been as shattering as watching her daughter Erin suffer. For two years, Susan lived in the household of her daughter and son-in-law David, helping with the infant twins and a toddler. During this time Erin had five spinal surgeries, radiation, and was in excruciating pain. Susie often fell into bed at night too exhausted to do anything but cry out to God with tears and anguish. She had nearly reached despair when, one night, she woke in the darkness to the sounds of a hymn echoing in her heart.

> Joyful, joyful, we adore Thee,
> God of glory, Lord of love;
> Hearts unfold like flowers before Thee,
> Praising Thee their sun above.
> Melt the clouds of sin and sadness,
> Drive the dark of doubt away;
> Giver of immortal gladness,
> Fill us with the light of day![11]

For Susie, a professional musician, nothing could have so soothed her soul like the music of an old hymn, and no words could have been a greater gift. She phoned me later that day and asked me to find the hymn and read her the other verses. Together, long distance, we cried about the goodness of God, beautifully and majestically delivered in the form of a song.

Erin isn't well yet. Her pain is still often excruciating, at times controlled to a manageable level with a small device surgically implanted in her abdomen, through which drugs are injected into her spinal column. She continues to live with paralysis and the weakness associated with radiation and nausea brought on by large doses of morphine.

Susie moved back home recently, but she often stays a few days with Erin and David when the realities of Erin's disability are overwhelming. During a recent visit to help out, God gave Susan a new song in the night. I listened as, over the phone, across the miles, she sang softly, sweetly:

> Like a River Glorious
> Is God's perfect peace,
> Over all victorious,
> In its bright increase.
> Perfect yet it floweth
> Fuller every day,
> Perfect yet it groweth
> Deeper all the way.

She struggled to sing through her tears as she reached this phrase in the second verse:

> Not a surge of worry,
> Not a shade of care
> Not a blast of hurry
> Touch the spirit there.[12]

"'Stayed upon Jehovah.' What a precious gift. That song and those precious words just flood my mind through the day and night," she wrote me later. "I've never experienced this before this season [of suffering], which began months ago. It is very unconscious on my part and I am taken by surprise by it, yet comforted."

Love of a Father

Not all our catastrophes come unbidden. Sometimes we invite them. Arrogance, disbelief, rebellion, and sometimes the actions that emerge out of our raw immaturity send us careening into disasters of our own making. What then?

Can we still bank on the goodness of God?

With all my heart I beg, yes, please! But sometimes, oftentimes, in guilt and embarrassment, drenched in my own self-made dilemma, I wonder what I can expect from God. Dare I hope He will be good to me?

But the truth of the life of Christ, the testimony of His words and His incarnation tell us this: When we are most aware of our "undeservedness," it seems God is most delighted to astonish us with His goodness.

When our son, Matt, was a teenager and the proud owner of a Jeep Wrangler, he and his friends used to spend weekends going "mudding." They set out across the Texas plains, caravan style, in their trucks and four-wheel-drive Jeeps, in search of the steepest, rockiest, muddiest patches of terrain they could find and then challenged each other to the supreme test. In most instances, if one car got stuck, another was able to pull it out. But one Saturday, the muddy creek was too much for Matt's Jeep. After several tries, the boys conceded defeat. It was time to call on help from a higher power. It was time to call Dad.

The boys trekked to a house about a mile from the creek and called us. My husband, Ken, answered the phone. I could tell it was something about the boys. He grabbed a notepad, jotted down some instructions—something about an outcropping off to the east side of a county road, follow it to a ravine, look off to the left. I dug through the phone book, gave Ken the number for a towing company, and listened while he repeated the same vague directions to a dispatcher. Moments later we headed off in search of the stranded boys.

We found a herd of muddy, chagrined teenagers sitting on a boulder near a rushing creek. It didn't take Ken long to agree that, yes, they needed a tow truck.

"What's it going to cost, Dad?" Matt asked.

"About eighty bucks," Ken answered.

Matt winced. His buddies ducked their heads.

"I'm sorry, Dad. We didn't know the creek was so deep. We couldn't see the rocks underwater. Once it got hung up, we couldn't get any traction."

Ken nodded. Then he reached into his pocket and pulled out a ten-dollar bill. "Here," he said, handing me the money and his car keys. "See if you can find a gas station anywhere close. You boys thirsty?" he called to Matt's friends.

Several astonished faces looked at Ken.

This was not what they had expected. Shouting, a scolding maybe, but not an offer of refreshment.

Matt grinned at his dad. I took drink orders and drove away. When I returned, Ken was sitting on the boulder with the boys, waiting for the tow truck to arrive and listening to the details of their adventure.

Later, Matt told us his friends had been amazed at Ken's composure. None of the other boys wanted to call their fathers. It was too risky for them, the danger of being humiliated and hollered at was too great. "I'd have been paying for this mess, one way or another, for the rest of my life," one boy said.

"I knew I could call you, Dad," Matt told us. "I didn't want to have to, but I knew I could. I knew you wouldn't go ballistic on me. I knew you'd help."

Matt knew his dad.

He knew that, in a crisis, in the midst of catastrophe, his father could be depended upon to help, not hurt. To rescue him, not renounce him.

I tell this story, not to brag on our parenting skills— both our children could tell you we've made more than our share of stupid mistakes (ask Matt about the day he lost his Roy Rogers holster and gun set). I tell it to illustrate the point that it is no small thing to discover that, when we are in the throes of crises, even our self-made ones, the goodness of a father can astonish.

Matt will never forget the goodness of his dad the day catastrophe struck when he and his friends took on a swollen Texas creek.

God is good, too. And it is no small thing to discover that, even when we are thrashing about in consequences we deserve, He is better than the best human father could ever imagine being. We can expect Him to astonish us with His goodness.

David wrote this Psalm, "Many, O LORD my God, are the wonders you have done. The things you planned for us no one can recount to you; were I to speak and tell of them, they would be too many to declare" (40:5).

The prodigal son returning to his father discovered him to be more welcoming, more full of goodness than he could have dared to expect.

Brother Jesus

Peter, after denying Christ, discovered Jesus anxious to restore their relationship, anxious to see Peter rid of his guilt and self-hatred. Relentlessly, He pursued Peter until Peter understood that his failure did not render him useless to the kingdom of God, useless to the Savior, and undesirable as a friend.

The older I get, the longer I live with my sin nature, the more I love this account of Jesus and His impetuous disciple.

The other day I was walking around the lake in my neighborhood, beating myself up for a recent failure, when suddenly Goodness broke into my consciousness. I knew Jesus was asking, "Jan, do you love Me?"

My answer was less than He deserved—it always will

be—but instead of turning away from me in disgust, I heard Him say, "Feed My sheep."

The enormity of this experience of grace cannot be adequately expressed in words. It defies everything we think about how the world should work, about how we should treat one another, and ourselves, when we've failed. It speaks to the feelings of dread and fear and loss that always accompany sin. In those three words, "feed My sheep," Jesus releases us from bondage to guilt, to shame, to futility, and the fear of being ostracized. He sums up redemption for us in the goodness of those words, setting us free from the penalty of our sin, and offering us a renewed relationship, which is not based upon anything we've ever done or ever will do.

Wherever Jesus encountered people, He encountered their catastrophes of sin and sadness and broken relationships. Where they expected revulsion, rebuke, or rejection, He offered them friendship and consolation, welcome and redemption.

A Roman soldier, the despised enemy of Jesus' own people, suddenly glimpsed infinite goodness when Jesus agreed to heal his child. Against a backdrop of national hate and personal cruelty, the goodness of Jesus shone brightly.

Jesus startled the tax collectors, thieves, and cheats, with dinner invitations! Our American culture understands fast food and potlucks, but we can't begin to comprehend the significance of Jesus sharing a meal with someone like Zacchaeus.

Brennan Manning wrote:

> In the East, to share a meal with someone is a symbol of peace, trust, brotherhood, and forgiveness; the shared table is a shared life. To say to an Orthodox

> Jew, "I would like to have dinner with you," is under-
> stood as "I would like to enter into friendship with
> you." . . . It did not escape the Pharisees' attention
> that Jesus meant to befriend the rabble. He was
> not only breaking the law, he was destroying
> the very structure of Jewish society! . . .
> But Zacchaeus, not too hung up on respectability,
> was overwhelmed with joy.[13]

God's goodness surprises us, doesn't it? We are astonished by it. How well George MacDonald expressed this
truth when he wrote, "While we who are evil would die to
give our children bread to eat, we are not certain that the
only Good in the universe will give us anything of what
we desire."[14]

Savior in Suffering

Nowhere is the goodness of God displayed more visibly,
more powerfully than on the cross. We find Jesus concerned for the care and well-being of His mother; Jesus
calling for the Father to forgive those who had hung Him
there; Jesus reaching out to the villain dying beside Him,
offering redemption in response to faith; and finally,
Jesus, dying for the sin of the world.

Stephen Charnock wrote that "the whole gospel is
nothing but one entire mirror of divine goodness."[15]

Dallas Willard makes it still more clear:

> Because of Christ's death for me and his continuing
> graces, I know that God is good, and I am thrilled
> with the hope that God's goodness and greatness
> will serve as the basis of my own existence
> as well as of everything else.[16]

God is good, totally, through and through. And because He is transcendent, His goodness is better than any definition of goodness we could ever write. Those who know this best are those who have hurt the worst and relied on God for comfort. These are the ones who have lost the most, and leaned on God for His sufficiency, those who have encountered painful catastrophes and trusted God to be faithful and just.

David, hiding in the wilderness of Judah, cried, "Thy lovingkindness is better than life" (Psalm 63:3 KJV).

It is impossible to read Paul's epistles and not hear the ring of praise for God's goodness—even when the writer is in chains. Praise because God has been sufficient, because God has sent friends to minister to Paul, because Paul has all the things he needs, even in prison. Praise because, no matter how bad Paul's circumstances may be, God's goodness continues to enfold him. It is no wonder Paul, more than any of the other New Testament writers, tells us to rejoice and give thanks in all things. He experienced the goodness of God in seemingly impossible circumstances, and his testimony is this: God's goodness never fails.

God delights in displaying His goodness to His children when they are suffering. Their stories of His goodness almost defy the tools of language. They have come to know Him more intimately and have felt His goodness administered in ways they never expected. They have learned to recognize and treasure His touch in surprising and incalculable ways.

Trembling, whimpering, these words find God's heart: "O Lord, dare we imagine thee as good as we hope thou art?"[17]

All That Is Left

Dallas Willard wrote, "If we are not living the great drama of goodness in God's kingdom, sensuality through the body is all that is left under our 'kingdom.'"[18]

All around me I see heartbreaking examples of individuals who, because they are not convinced of the goodness of God, are looking for solace, for escape, in sensuality. Sometimes, I see myself among them, seeking relief from emotional turmoil in a carton of ice cream, or a pleasing fantasy that will let me remove myself, temporarily, artificially, from the place and circumstances that are causing me distress and pain.

That is, in fact, all that is left to us if we reject the goodness of God.

If we reject the truth of God's goodness, we must comfort ourselves with something else—food, fleeting moments of fun (at all levels of extremes), or fantasy.

We will try to dull the spirit's agony with pornography, soft or hard, real or virtual.

We will seek to escape our pain with drugs, or exercise, or any number of obsessive behaviors that, by teasing the body with temporal pleasure, convince the soul of a false sense of well-being.

But always, the "drug of choice" wears off, leaving us emptier and sadder and more confused than before, and ever more dependent upon the wrong things for relief, because "habit renders the pleasures of vanity and excitement and flippancy at once less pleasant and harder to forgo."[19]

Lost in an ever-deepening spiral of addictive pursuits, we find ourselves more and more miserable, more and more obsessive, and more and more unsatisfied by the very things for which we would sell our souls.

Unless we choose to live the great drama of God's

goodness, in spite of pain and difficulty, we have no option but to chase after more adventures, taking more risks, seeking more activities, more additives, more relationships that numb our pain for a moment. And all the while, Jesus stands before us, offering us communion with Himself, fellowship with the infinite God! And the gifts of goodness and mercy and tender care.

Not put off by our confusion and the chaos of our lives, He yearns to draw us into His arms and whisper words of comfort and healing. He yearns to show us the significance of our suffering. He yearns to dazzle us with divine wonders.

Messengers of Hope

Life is a mess most of the time. Nowhere does it seem messier than in a hospital waiting room.

I arrived early, before my loved one who would be having surgery, and staked out my space in the already crowded waiting area. I opened my notebook and began writing, "Lord, this is so scary. I wish a pastor was here to pray with me."

But it wasn't my surgery, and it wasn't my place to line up clergy for the day. I would have to respect the wishes of my loved ones and their desire for privacy, trusting God to be present to us in whatever way He would choose.

The Spirit of God whispered to my soul, "He shall give his angels charge over thee, to keep thee in all thy ways."

It was the old King James Version of Psalm 91:11 that I had memorized as a child. With tears in my eyes, I jotted the verse in my notebook. Then, beneath it I wrote, "Lord, I'll be watching for your angels today. Don't let me miss a one."

Moments later, Neal Jeffrey, the pastor who had only six weeks earlier preached at Ken's mother's funeral, stepped off the elevator and walked into the waiting room. He was making a routine hospital call, but for me there was nothing routine about his presence. He asked why we were there, and then said, "Well, come on, let's go pray!"

No one could have better served our family that day than this man, who knew us all, from the youngest to the oldest. Over the years, he had shown up on the sidelines on Friday nights to cheer for our son, Matt, during high school football games. He had taught and encouraged Molly during her years in the youth group. He had ministered to Ken's dad during his months in the hospital. And, finally, he had buried Ken's beloved mother.

And now, here he stood, a "messenger to transcendence"—that's what Eugene Peterson calls angels.[20] That day, I heard the message of God's transcendent goodness, a clarion call to trust ringing loud and clear over the noise and confusion and the droning sounds of CNN that played on a television in the corner of a hospital waiting room.

Confident of Goodness

David wrote, "I am still confident of this: I will see the goodness of the LORD in the land of the living. Wait for the LORD; be strong and take heart and wait for the LORD" (Psalm 27:13–14).

The Hebrew lexicon makes these verses even more precious, for "confident" means *firm*, and "wait" means *to expect*. David's words become my solace as I draw on this meaning: I am firm in my expectation of God's goodness.

On some days I'm more "firm" than on others.

Only recently, burdened with an overpowering sense of guilt and battling self-hatred, I wondered, Does the

Good Shepherd who promises to gently lead those who are with young have any goodness for an aging, cantankerous ewe? I scanned Isaiah's fortieth chapter and found this:

> *God doesn't come and go. God lasts. . . .*
> *He energizes those who get tired,*
> *gives fresh strength to dropouts.*
> *For even young people tire and drop out,*
> *young folk in the prime stumble and fall.*
> *But those who wait upon God get fresh strength.*
> *They spread their wings and soar like eagles.*
> *They run and don't get tired,*
> *they walk and don't lag behind.*
>
> —ISAIAH 40:28–31 THE MESSAGE

God lasts!

I love that!

When my strength gives out, God's lasts. When my guilt lingers, His grace outlasts it.

Because He is good.

Yes, there will be days when in our troubled circumstances we can't imagine being firm about anything, when the only thing we're certain about is our miserable condition. Our expectations will be filled with dread, not hope, and with the ancient cynics we will ask, "How can anything good come out of Nazareth?"

Always God answers us with the same message: "Nothing is too hard for Me." Impossibilities are His specialty. Madame Guyon wrote, "Never try to imagine what God will do. There is no way God will ever fit into your concepts."[21]

He will exceed our expectations; He will surpass them.

"We cannot have too much faith in so good and faith-

ful a Friend, who will never fail us in this world or in the
next."[22]

 Tracking Grace

> PEOPLE WHO HOPE NEVER KNOW WHAT'S COMING NEXT.
> THEY EXPECT IT IS GOING TO BE GOOD, BECAUSE GOD IS
> GOOD. EVEN WHEN DISASTERS OCCUR, PEOPLE OF HOPE
> LOOK FOR HOW GOD WILL USE EVIL FOR GOOD.[23]
> —EUGENE PETERSON

They cried to you and were saved;
in you they trusted and were not disappointed.
—PSALM 22:5

1. What illusions about God might prevent you
   from believing the truth about His goodness?

2. What does it mean to you that God's goodness
   has no shadows?

3. In what ways have you been comforted by God's "having-beenness"?

4. Record an instance when the goodness of God took you by surprise.

5. Write a prayer or poem of thanksgiving for God's goodness.

HOLINESS IS A GLORIOUS
PERFECTION BELONGING TO
THE NATURE OF GOD. . . .
THIS IS HIS GREATEST TITLE
OF HONOR. . . . HOLINESS
HIS BEAUTY.[1]

STEPHEN CHARNOCK

Day and night they never stop saying:
Holy, holy, holy is the Lord God Almighty,
who was, and is, and is to come.

—REVELATION 4:8

CHAPTER FIVE

The First Necessary Truth

GOD IS HOLY
AND I AM NOT

The villain knew his guilt. He was dying because of it. There was nothing he could do but hang helplessly, waiting for the relief of unconsciousness. What lay beyond that, when death stopped his heart, he could only dread with every pained breath he drew.

He would suffer a ghastly death—nailed to a tree, stared at in ghoulish curiosity by his countrymen. Soldiers would break his arms and legs to rush him into whatever black abyss awaited him. He would go in agony and shame, knowing it was his due.

The moment for hope had long since passed.

Until Jesus was hoisted up to die alongside him.

While tormentors sneered and mocked the one labeled "King of the Jews," a thief who deserved to die said, "He's not guilty, but we are."

Every time I read the story of this criminal, I am startled by the depth of his understanding. Minds overstuffed with theology debate great concepts and obscure points of eschatology, but there, hanging naked and condemned, a man of no consequence grasped the most basic, essential theological truth every individual must deal with: God is holy and I'm not.

If ever we are to experience grace, we must grapple with the holiness of God.

We must grapple with the reality of our own unholiness.

We must grapple with the reality of sin.

Blazing, Not Banal

Sin is the one catastrophe that we all share.

While we may not all experience chemotherapy, or bankruptcy, or any one of a number of tragedies and losses that we consider catastrophic, what I share with you, and you share with me is the horror of sin and its consequences.

If ever we are going to experience the depths of God's grace, our first confession must be the thief's words, *Lord, You're holy and I'm not.*

For the thief, it was an easy call. The courts of his land had found him guilty; he made no excuses. The evidence was indisputable, the verdict just.

For most of us, it's not so easy.

Our crimes are not always so obvious.

And our view of God is often skewed, our idea of holiness vague.

And who wants to think about holiness anyway? Who really wants to spend time considering such a distant, off-putting concept? If topics can be literally too hot to handle, this one promises to scorch and singe—"Holiness is not banal. Holiness is blazing."[2]

If you're like me, you're not sure you can stand the heat.

But our desire for grace, our unspoken, often unrecognized yearning for the incomparable gift of intimacy with God requires us to deal with His holiness. Of all His attributes, this is "the only attribute of God that is raised to the third power;" God's name is qualified by the adjective "holy" in the Old Testament more often than all the other qualities combined.[3]

Dare we ignore this truth?

The Starting Place

It sounds fearsome, doesn't it?

Holiness suggests anger, fury, terror. The mere word sends most of us into varying states of discomfort. So that's where we must begin—with an understanding of what is meant by the word "holy."

Sam Storms helps me here. Writing about God's holiness, he said, "God is in a class all by Himself. . . . 'A cut above' the rest. That is what God is, to an infinite degree. . . . Holiness is a reference to transcendence."[4]

If I look around at the messes that litter my life, my community, my world—damaged relationships, desperate heartbreak, evil endeavors—I have to say the one thing I most need right now is someone who is "a cut above."

I need someone who is not mired in messes and locked in chaos.

I need someone the prophets describe as separate, distinct, uncommon.

Samuel wrote, "There is no one holy like the LORD" (1 Samuel 2:2; see 6:20).

Isaiah wrote of the "Holy One of Jacob . . . the God of Israel," of whom all will "stand in awe" (29:23).

Over and over again, the prophets ask, "Who is like you, O God?" And the resounding answer is always, "No one!"

God is unique, set apart from all the ideas we may come up with to describe Him. We cannot fully capture His essence. Because He is totally, completely "other."

This is the most basic definition of holiness.

No wonder we shrink from the idea of it. It suggests a vast distance that we can never connect with. But so great is the holiness, the "otherness" of God, that "His infinite loftiness . . . does not entail His aloofness. God is great, but He is not geographically distant."[5]

This is the God we so desperately need: Emanuel, God *with* us; God, the unique "One and Only," the Other that supercedes anything we can ever imagine; the One who enters into our chaos with us, but cannot be ensnared by it; the One who enters my geography with its sin and squalor, bringing with Him uncommon integrity and moral perfection.

This is the God that the thief implored.

Even in His nakedness, in His agony, Jesus' holiness blazed. Through a blur of pain and despair, the dying thief could see that Jesus was "Other," fully God, perfect in moral excellence, perfect in integrity. Jesus was His only hope.

I remember the day I saw, through the blur of my tears, that Jesus was my only hope.

I was twelve. Some crazy cult had predicted that the world would end on February 12, 1962. Only those who put on white robes and went to stand on a desert hill somewhere outside Phoenix would be saved.

My only robe was pink chenille and Phoenix was three

hours away. I wasn't *fully* convinced that the world would come to an end at midnight, but I was frightened enough to cry alone in my bed that night and to confess that I wasn't ready to die if it did.

I knew the sinner's prayer. My parents often had told me I prayed it when I was about four or five, but I didn't remember praying it. What I did remember was my selfishness toward my sisters and the lies I had told my parents and my Brownie Scout leader so I could quit the troop.

I remembered being jealous of my best friend because she was an only child.

I remembered being a brat in Sunday school because my dad was the chairman of the deacon board and I could get away with it.

I remembered pretending I was sick so I could stay home from school.

I remembered, and felt full of dread, because I knew I was not holy and God is.

My life could be over in a matter of hours, I thought, and like the thief, I cried out to God.

I mark that day as the day I confessed my unholiness and grabbed hold of God's.

I mark that day as the day Jesus said, "Don't worry, you will live with Me someday in paradise."

Only One who is holy can make such a promise.

The Irony of Holiness

It is only the first of many promises God makes to us when we confess our sin and accept by faith His gift of eternal life.

He also promises to *make us holy*.

Moses, writing in Leviticus, gives Israel this word from God, "I am the LORD, who makes you holy" (20:7).

The Hebrew lexicon tells me that this is a kind of ceremonial declaration that God makes. It has nothing to do with the actions or behaviors of the people—it has everything to do with the intent of God.

In declaring Israel holy, He was in essence saying, "You belong to Me. I am responsible for you. You are unique, distinct among the people of the earth."

In Hebrews, we find that God said, "Both the one who makes men holy, and those who are made holy are of the same family. So Jesus is not ashamed to call them brothers" (2:11).

This is astounding truth: God, who is perfect and excellent in all He does, chooses for Himself a "ragamuffin" people, a foolish, filthy, frail people. He declares them unique, set apart, and ceremonially clean because of the sacrificial death of His Son, Jesus, whose blood washes away their sin. And then He welcomes them as sons and daughters and designates them as "family."

Family He is not ashamed of.

This is not just amazing, it is staggering.

The holiday season is in full swing as I write this, and tales of family gatherings past are everywhere—the happy tales, the sad tales, the hysterically funny tales, the ones about the embarrassing relatives that show up and bring chaos into the festivities—the relatives that bring shame into the household. There is one in every family.

You know what it's like to anticipate the upcoming holidays and dread the arrival of the one whose presence triggers instant shame and embarrassment. Maybe it's you—you're the one whose past failure and present ineptness bring embarrassment in through the front door.

Maybe it's a cousin, or a nephew, one who doesn't have as much education as the rest of the family. Maybe it's one whose marriage is a mess and the mess goes everywhere she goes. Maybe it's the teenager whose hair is fuchsia this year, or the child who has ADHD and puts everyone on edge. Maybe it's the loud uncle whose coarse manners make you ill at ease, or the grandmother who makes only subtle, faux efforts at hiding her disappointment that the gifts she received were less than her due.

Families can be the breeding places for shame.

But not the family of God.

This is the divine irony of infinite holiness: The God who is perfect in all His splendid manifestations, whose integrity is unimpeachable, throws open the door of the family estate and invites us in without being embarrassed by our weaknesses, our reputations, our appearances. He wraps His arms around us and declares loudly, "Look who's here! It's My child! I've got great plans for her life! She's special to Me! Welcome her—make room at the table!"

When I began this study on holiness, I never imagined I would find myself weeping in wonder, overwhelmed by awe at what the holiness of God means for me.

It means that even though I have lied and lived selfishly, been lazy, unkind, unfair, and unloving, rude, hypocritical and deliberately disobedient, a holy God isn't ashamed to call me family.

He welcomes me into a relationship as a source of joy, not shame.

Because He is not like anyone else I know.

He is not like any human family.

He is not like me, or you.

Like a presidential declaration that makes an alien a citizen, God declares that we are holy. But it is a bloody declaration. Through Jesus' death and resurrection, God addresses the catastrophe of our sin, our unholiness. He credits us with the perfection of Christ, and He "brands" us as a holy people—"special, set apart, called out of the world to the unthinkable destiny of eternal ecstasy in spiritual marriage to God almighty."[6]

We have nothing to do with it. We simply stand at the throne of grace and accept the truth of it.

But the living out of that holiness is a whole other matter.

Stabilized by Holiness

At times, I've envied the thief who died alongside Jesus—not the torment of his cruel death, but the immediacy of paradise.

Wouldn't it be great to utter the words of faith and be instantly translated into the perfection of heaven? Of course, on some days that's more appealing than on others. Every day, I'm aware of the unholiness of my life and all life around me, in spite of that declaration God made about me being legally and ceremonially holy, set apart, and distinct. I realize how much I am just like everyone else—criminals, all of us. I recognize how far short I fall of the holiness that Jesus displayed for me, the holiness He calls me to.

And the call is clear.

"But just as he who called you is holy, so be holy in all you do; for it is written: 'Be holy, because I am holy'" (1 Peter 1:15–16).

I know that there is now "no condemnation for those who are in Christ Jesus" (Romans 8:1). But still, sin has a presence in my life because home is here, not paradise, and I face catastrophes of my own making because of it every day.

"This is where I live—down here in the muck and mess," a friend told me as she talked about a heartbreaking disturbance in her family life.

It's where I live too. We're all right here together: sheep, all of us.

We wander in pastures where, no matter where we place a hoof, we're likely to step on a steaming pile. We're part of a flock of woolly creatures that fall over and can't get up without help. We are timid and foolish—we will suffer and die of thirst rather than risk the dangers of drinking from a stream that gurgles. We don't see well enough to recognize a wolf in sheep's clothing. And worst of all, we wander off.

The holiness, the integrity of the Shepherd is our only hope. His desire for our holiness is our safety.

> Christ is the Good Shepherd, but He keeps many terrible sheepdogs. . . . They have terrible fearful names . . . Pain, Fear, Anxiety, and Shame—sacred creatures those dogs, too, for they work the will of the Father.[7]

The will of the Father is this: that we know Him, know the perfection of His nature and the splendor of His character, and that we enjoy Him forever.

That "knowing" and "enjoying" is most often best learned through suffering; from having been nipped and nudged, chased and driven into the arms of the Shepherd by a terrible sheepdog.

"God is not mean," wrote Dallas Willard, "but he is dangerous."[8]

God is dangerous to our idea of what our lives should look like. Because He is holy—totally "other than" what we in our ignorance and finite imaginations might devise for ourselves; He is "other than" what the American dream is selling.

God is dangerous to our idea of how others should behave; of how others should treat us, how we should treat them.

He will pursue us with pain to convince us that our

true health and prosperity will only ever be found in an intimate relationship with Him.

He will let anxiety and fear loose for a while to gnaw at us until finally we collapse into the security of His arms where, cuddled against His heart, we can view the terrain of our lives and see that without Him it is barren.

He will release shame to attack us—the kind of shame that is our friend when it shows us the ugliness of our self-indulgence and rebellion; when it sends us running for the kindness and mercy of the Shepherd.

Holy, other, a cut above. God will not, He *cannot* leave His sheep to their own fate when He has pledged Himself to complete that which He has begun in them (see Philippians 1:6).

We are His "workmanship, created in Christ Jesus to do good works which God prepared in advance for us to do" (Ephesians 2:10).

Because He is holy, we can find rest in His arms and know the companionship of ferocious love, unrelenting mercy, and extravagant grace. It is the sound of a Holy God roaring after us, pursuing us in love. The destiny He has in store for us far surpasses the trifling pastimes we so blithely indulge in here and now.

Because He is "other than."

> Nothing is above Him, nothing beyond Him. Any
> motion in His direction is elevation for the creature;
> away from Him, descent. . . . As no one can promote
> Him, no one can degrade Him.[9]

God is above all things, all created beings, all matter, and all manner of things our imaginations could conjure.

But He is not above hurting us, if that is what His holiness demands.

Restoring the Ruins

Frederick Buechner wrote, "Anyone who has ever known him has known him perhaps better in the dark than anywhere else because it is in the dark where he seems to visit most often."[10]

When our vision of life is darkened by the blur of tears, when we're brokenhearted over our wanderings, God's visit may surprise us. We expect from God what we expect from ourselves (and those like us when we have wronged them)—derision, repulsion, rejection. But suddenly, in our darkness, the light of His holiness shines—*He is not like us!* And we hear David's reminder, "A broken and contrite heart, O God, you will not despise" (Psalm 51:17).

God loves a broken heart, a heart that sorrows over sin. Our shuddering sobs do not embarrass or disgust Him.

"The broken in heart are His beloved, His jewels," wrote John Bunyan.[11]

Through the prophet Isaiah, God says to us:

For this is what the high and lofty One says—he who lives forever, whose name is holy; "I live in a high and holy place but also with him who is contrite and lowly in spirit, to revive the spirit of the lowly, and to revive the heart of the contrite."

—Isaiah 57:15

Until that day when we see heaven and the glory of God with new eyes, we cannot possibly grasp the immensity of God's declaration in this verse. His holiness is high and lofty, far beyond us, but when we are heartbroken over our sin, He is closest to us.

The Hebrew word paints a picture of God moving in

to live with us, in our brokenness, to stabilize us. We're weak and damaged, tottering, on the verge of collapse. But He is holy, above us, and He is able to prop us up.

When we are honest about our sins, transparent, and authentic before God, He restores, revives, and brings the stability that we so desperately need. He honors our grief over sin with the perfection of His kind and compassionate presence.

The fact that we are declared holy, ceremonially, does not "shut out the presence of indwelling sin," wrote Bishop Ryle. "But it is the excellence of a holy man that he is not at peace with indwelling sin, as others are. . . . He hates it, mourns over it and longs to be free from it."[12]

For Christians who desire to know God and live in the reality of His holiness, not a day will pass that we will not be conscious of willfulness toward sin and rebellion in our lives. If it grieves us and breaks our hearts that we have sinned against the Father who loves us, not a day will pass without His reviving, redeeming presence to shape us and reassure us. His promise, "I am the LORD, who makes them holy," will ring joy in our souls (Leviticus 22:9).

This is my only hope, because left to myself I have no aptitude for personal holiness.

Not Natural for Us

Until my children reached high school, the one thing I dreaded above everything else in their academic careers was the announcement of the annual science fair. Every student under ninth grade had to submit a science project, no exceptions.

Now, our family is science challenged. Ken does have a first cousin on his father's side who is a rocket scientist (really!), but that gene doesn't swim in Ken's pool. Ken is, however, a brilliant businessman with a memory that would make an elephant look senile. Matt inherited his dad's business savvy; Molly has a mind for logic and the law, and I'm a word person, but none of us has an aptitude for science. It's outside the range of our natural abilities and interests.

Imagine our terror every year when we faced the rules for the science fair projects. I say "our" and "we" because it had to be a family project—not one of us was capable of working alone, regardless of the rules requiring it to be the student's project *alone*. We always read that regulation and shared a bitter, ironic laugh.

We scrambled for an idea, always feeling like we were working out of a vacuum. We had no designs of our own and no means of implementing a plan even if we'd been able to come up with a reasonable one! We looked for help from any source, and finally (usually at the last minute) handed in our best effort—always a simplistic, awkward family project like watching mold grow on a piece of bread. We breathed a sigh of relief if "we" passed. We had no illusions of winning anything or being recognized for brilliance. We just dreaded failure.

I have to confess that often the topic of personal holiness brings back all those old uncomfortable feelings of doomed inadequacy for me.

Like science, I have no aptitude for holiness. Does anyone? And so we're awkward, ill equipped. When the apostles and the prophets write, "Be holy," we feel our failure before we even begin our efforts.

What a miserable way to live.

To think of regimenting the hours of our day around a standard we can never achieve; to think of trying to build something (a holy life) that we can't even imagine designing, much less implementing!

And holiness *is* a family affair. It is a lifelong pursuit, directed by God our Father who gives us all the tools, all the insight, all the skill we will ever need to be holy.

Think of it like this: The Nobel Prize winner for scientific achievement is your dad. Imagine him leading you by the hand into the laboratory and promising to stay with you and teach you. Imagine him patiently working with you, encouraging you, correcting you, helping you discover amazing things. Imagine suddenly realizing that in all the time you've spent together it's not just science you've been learning—you've been spending time with your father, and learning to know him, learning to enjoy what he enjoys.

Imagine realizing that the joy of the relationship is more important to you than any project you might turn out. Imagine him declaring you brilliant because you finally get it! This was his intention all along!

Imagine it if you can.

Read it in Proverbs 9:10: "Knowledge of the Holy One is understanding."

Our English translation weakens the power of this verse. Read it like this:

> As you gain personal and experiential understanding of the majesty of God's holiness; as you are awed by the perfection of His nature, His "otherness," His uniqueness; as you begin to grasp just how magnificent God is in all His moral excellence and splendid beauty, then and only then can you lay claim to discernment, prudence, intelligence, insight and skill.[13]

God is saying, get to know Me and you will gain rich spiritual insight and skills for holy living.

To me, this is life-changing truth. It invites us into the

laboratory of life with God, to live and work alongside Him. The goal is not to turn out a perfect specimen of holy living in this lifetime; the goal is to learn to know God, to learn to treasure the things He treasures; to learn to love Him in response to His love.

But expect to see changes in your life! Because you can't spend that kind of time with someone and not be affected by his character, his integrity.

Expect to discover that your ideas about life will begin to change; you will begin to think differently, to act differently. You will begin to reflect the "otherness" of your Father, your Teacher. You will begin to understand and appreciate what God tells you about life, and habits, and love, and obedience.

"He who most entirely agrees with God, he is the most holy man," wrote a nineteenth-century saint.[14]

Holiness, for the child of God, is learning to live in agreement with God, agreeing that His ways are best, and relying on the power of His indwelling Spirit to enable us to make the choices that reflect His integrity.

Journeying with God

Gary Thomas wrote that "true holiness has at its root an overwhelming passion for the one true and holy God, not for rules, principles, or standards. This holiness is relational."[15]

God spare us from letting the pursuit of our own personal holiness cause us to become perfectionistic, boring, and persnickety about trivial matters—people "whose goodness has become cheerless and finicky, a technique for working off [our] own guilts, a gift with no love in it which neither deceives nor benefits any for long."[16]

Such "holiness," if it can be called that, is a sham. It

produces a false life, a false self that is at odds with the kind of transparency God calls us to.

God, because of His integrity, wants us to learn to be truthful, real, not fussy and meticulous. He wants us to live honestly and humbly before Him.

And He will use any means in the laboratory of life to teach us that. John Bunyan wrote:

> He will wound them that He may heal them. . . . If He
> will have them, He must fetch them, follow them,
> catch them, lame them, even break their bones,
> or else he shall not save them.[17]

In good times and tough times, through hours, weeks, of being chased by "terrible sheepdogs," He will show us that His ways are best, His words are true, His love is great, and His faithfulness is absolute.

We must learn, and daily *relearn,* to agree with God.

And that will set us apart from those who don't.

It won't make us perfect, as some might define holiness. It won't make us bulletproof, as the chaos in our lives will testify.

We will continually disappoint ourselves and those watching us, hoping for our perfection, but we must remind ourselves that "God does not want perfect performances but loving persons; He is not a stage manager but a lover. We learn by the mistakes we make and the sufferings they bring."[18]

Holiness is not a plateau we arrive at; it is a journey we embark on, by faith, taking one step at a time, often stumbling, often mistaken in our idea of what holiness should look like. Those wiser than us remind us that there are no overnight successes, and we would be wise to heed them.

Brother Lawrence warns us not to try to "go faster than grace allows. One does not become holy all at once."[19]

First Necessary Truth

"The way to get to know the first necessary thing about ourselves, that we are sinners in need of forgiveness, is to get to know the all-holy, all-just, uncompromising, unbribable character of God," wrote Peter Kreeft.[20]

This is a hard truth, but the thief on the cross got it. Seeing the all-holy God, he saw the "first necessary truth" about himself—the truth we all must see about ourselves: that God is holy and we are not.

God cannot be bribed or coerced into overlooking our sin—what would we offer Him that He does not already own as Creator of all things? With what could we threaten the King of Kings?

Our first, most needful truth is found in the thief's confession: You are holy and I am not.

Our plea is the same as the thief's: Remember me!

Our comfort and joy are in His answer: Today you have come home, and I will never let you go.

The Great Exchange

Sin is our greatest catastrophe. Yet grace meets us there and by faith our eyes are opened to the panorama of possibilities that lie outside of our natural abilities.

We encounter the holiness of God for the first time when we understand that we are sinners. We see ourselves as the unholy creatures that we are, and God says, "You don't have to stay here in this pit of filth and longing and despair. I'll haul you out and give you new life, new options, new opportunities you never before imagined!"

In faith, we accept the grip of God on our lives. We release the weight of our sin, letting ourselves fall hard on the strength of His grace, and we find ourselves loved and rescued, redeemed and remade.

The stench of the pit is washed away and we discover an aptitude we never had before! We have ideas about living that come from the giver of life who is now our Father; we have passion and enthusiasm we never had before. We are no longer living in a vacuum, devoid of all concepts of holiness. Because we are now and forever declared holy ourselves.

This is theology that should give joy and confidence to all of us who ever sat in a church pew and felt the pain of inadequacy and ineptness as the preacher preached and the choir sang and members all around bowed their heads in a show of holiness we couldn't feel.

This is theology that should turn our despair into dancing. Regardless of the inadequacies others may see in us, God's searing holiness has marked us, branding us as His holy ones.

We are not left to struggle after holiness on our own.

God enables us and empowers us. Paul's words comfort me when I read that the *Lord* will "strengthen your hearts so that you will be blameless and holy" (1 Thessalonians 3:13).

God transforms.

He is dogged in His determination to accomplish this. He will use any and all means.

The One Constant

I was shocked to hear myself called a hypocrite. Shocked, and devastated. I had hurt my friend and was deeply sorry about it, but as I grieved and prayed, I began to see that there was more here than the consequences of a few careless words I had tossed flippantly into a conversation.

I realized that I'd been appalled at the idea that hypocrisy could be found in me. And that, of course, exposed the whole iceberg of pride that lay under the surface.

It was a miserable week. Added to the catastrophe of my pride, my parents became ill, and I was worried about them. As if that weren't enough, other dearly loved family members were struck with a sudden, unexpected heartbreak. Making things worse, I felt certain I had caused deep disappointment to well-loved relatives on the other side of the family tree. And the final blow: Ken flew off to blizzard-laden Philadelphia, leaving me home alone for the week with a sixty-pound dog that decided the family room sofa would make a great midday snack.

There, in the middle of all that mess, I faced a publishing deadline, a blank computer screen, and the urgency of writing a chapter on the topic of holiness. Nothing could have been less inviting. But as I dug in and studied, praying and weeping much of the time, I began to see that when life is messy, the holiness of God can be my sweet comfort.

His holiness is the guarantee that everything else He says about Himself will be true.

Because integrity is the core strength of any relationship.

The unimpeachable character of God is my safety. Because of the perfection of His nature, His splendid moral excellence, I have every reason to trust Him and run to Him for help.

I can rely on Him to be above the chaos of my life. I can trust His Word—that He will reach down and rescue me when in faith I call for His help. There is no one higher or more perfect.

All God's dealings with us will reflect His holiness. All His dealings will reflect His perfect integrity.

Because He is holy, the greatest good He can offer us is an encounter with His excellence. The greatest honor He can bestow on us is the reality of an ever-deepening, never-ending intimacy with Him.

The Foundation of Faith

"Show me Your glory," Moses asked of God.

Show me Your splendor, Your majesty, all the things that make up Your holiness, Your "otherness"—it was an audacious request from one God called the humblest of men.

God agreed. He hid Moses in the cleft of a rock and let him see the back side of His blazing holiness as He passed by—holiness that would have consumed Moses without tons of granite to shield him.

I think about the fiery heat of God's holiness, and I want to run for the shelter of the rocks too. But then I hear Jesus say, "I am the Rock. I am the Cornerstone."

I see Moses take off his sandals when Yahweh speaks to him from the flames of a burning bush, and again, holiness would terrify. I feel compelled to slip off my leopard-print house shoes, and when I look down, I see Jesus at my feet with a basin and a towel.

Where Jesus is, there is holiness. Nothing less than the perfect integrity of the Father, full of grace and truth, but shrouded in human form so that we will not run *away* from Him in terror, but to Him in faith, expecting welcome. So that when we look down in shame, we see the smile of His upturned face.

God's splendor of heart is our only hope.

When we yearn for peace, solace, and safety in our catastrophes, it will only ever be found in the reality of God's integrity, in His holiness. It will only ever be found

in Jesus, "the holy One of God who shared life with un-holy sinners."[21]

His integrity is the sinner's only security.

Unless He is holy, His love will be suspect.

Unless He is holy, unlike all the ideas I might have of common integrity, His promises are worthless, His assurances are nothing more than pretty poet's words, His presence not a comfort but a threat.

Unless God is holy, there is no safe place in all the universe.

For all of us caught in the catastrophe of sin, the holiness of God is our best and only hope.

"He has made you sorry on earth," wrote Bunyan, "that you might rejoice in heaven—all this because He has a mind to make you laugh."[22]

When all the books on theology have been written and read, and all the great theses have been argued and laid to rest, the dying thief's words of faith will remain the essential truth for all of us: "Lord, You are holy and I am not."

And Jesus' promise of home in paradise will be our certainty only because He is holy.

Nothing else can make it true.

TRACKING GRACE

HE MUST BE AN ARTIST INDEED AT BELIEVING
WHO CAN COME TO GOD UNDER HIS GUILT AND HORROR,
AND PLEAD IN FAITH THAT THE SACRIFICES OF GOD
ARE A BROKEN HEART, SUCH AS HE HAS,
AND THAT A BROKEN AND A CONTRITE SPIRIT
GOD WILL NOT DESPISE.[23]

—JOHN BUNYAN

But now that you have been set free from sin and have become slaves to God, the benefit you reap leads to holiness, and the result is eternal life. For the wages of sin is death, but the gift of God is eternal life in Christ Jesus our Lord.
—ROMANS 6:22–23

1. Why do you think knowing that we are sinners is the "the first necessary truth" about ourselves?

2. What, if any, catastrophe has caused you to consider the holiness of God? What was your response?

3. What is your response to the idea of God desiring your holiness?

4. What does it mean to you to think that His holiness is the very reason why you can trust Him?

WE CANNOT HAVE A RIGHT
CONCEPTION OF GOD
UNLESS WE THINK OF HIM AS
ALL-POWERFUL, AS WELL AS
ALL-WISE. HE WHO CANNOT
DO WHAT HE WILL AND
PERFORM ALL HIS PLEASURE
CANNOT BE GOD.[1]

ARTHUR PINK

The LORD is my light and my salvation—
whom shall I fear?
The LORD is the stronghold of my life—
of whom shall I be afraid?

—PSALM 27:1

CHAPTER SIX

Our Safe Refuge
GOD'S OMNI-ATTRIBUTES

I love the Old Testament story of Elisha's servant who stepped out into the cool of the morning and discovered that an enemy army of horses and chariots had surrounded the city during the night. Elisha was their target, but they would kill anyone else who got in their way.

You can hear the panic in the servant's question, "What are we going to do?"

Elisha answered, "Don't be afraid. Those who are with us are more than those who are with them" (see 2 Kings 6:8–18).

I can just imagine the servant looking around, eyes blinking, speech sputtering in confusion and terror. And then, Elisha prayed and asked God to open his servant's eyes so he could see God's armies swarming the countryside. Everywhere he looked, the servant saw horses and blazing chariots.

I could use a view of flaming chariots at times, couldn't you?

We wouldn't mind if God showed up with fire and snorting stallions and chariots manned by angelic warriors who would tear into whatever was disturbing our peace. But ask around—such dramatic displays of God's power are rare these days.

And yet, God's incomparable power is still at work.

And like Elisha, Paul prayed that our eyes will be opened to see all that we have reason to hope for as the children of God; all that we have reason to celebrate—the incomparable power of God is at work for us who believe; in fact, Paul the apostle wrote that God's power "is like the working of his mighty strength, which he exerted in Christ when he raised him from the dead and seated him at his right hand in the heavenly realms, far above all rule and authority, power and dominion, and every title that can be given, not only in the present age but in the one to come" (Ephesians 1:18–21).

And not His power only, but perfect knowledge and wisdom that direct His power so that His majestic character and His extravagant grace can be seen throughout the universe, in all places, at all times, for all time.

It all comes together: God's omnipotence, His omniscience, and His omnipresence.

It has to.

If God were powerful, but absent, what would be the point of our trust?

Would we dare rely on a being who claimed great power but had limited data and no discernment? Our fates would be no less safe in the hands of a professional wrestler.

A god who is wise and well-informed yet weak and inadequate could do us no more good than a scholarly neighbor.

For God to be worthy of our worship, He must be all-powerful, all knowing, wise, and always everywhere present at the same time.

Anything less would be less than God claims to be. Anything less would be less than we need, and less would mean there is no safety for us, no security, no hope, and no help for us ever, anytime, anyplace.

No Place beyond Him

No matter where you turn, God is there.

Tozer wrote, "There is no place beyond Him for anything to be. God is our environment as the sea is to the fish and air to the bird." This, he adds, is the "central truth that gives meaning to all other truths and imparts supreme value to [the believer's] life."[2]

David said it like this in Psalm 139:5–6: "You hem me in—behind and before; you have laid your hand upon me. Such knowledge is too wonderful for me, too lofty for me to attain."

David is boggled by the truth of God's omnipresence, that it is impossible to be anyplace that is beyond God's reach! David seemed to struggle for words to express his amazement.

Some of us may be less than thrilled.

The legalist will always shrink from the truth of an omnipresent God. Who wants a divine cop always present, hovering about, just waiting for us to mess up? And because we are sinners and prone to messing up at any moment, a legalist perceives that God's displeasure is only a small misstep away.

I remember learning the Sunday school chorus that warns little hands, little eyes, little ears to be careful, because God is watching. This wasn't an appealing thought to me as I was growing up. I imagined God's grim expression, His hot wrath just waiting to explode and consume me if my eyes, ears, or hands misbehaved.

I imagined God like a stern warden, striding the hallways of my life, watching me with narrowed eyes. Who would want to run to this God at the first sign of trouble? This is a God to run *away* from.

But the theology of God's omnipresence tells us that there is no place we can flee from Him. He never sleeps or even takes a nap—we cannot hope for even a brief respite from His presence (see Psalm 121:4).

Even so, we often try to hide because we haven't grasped that God does not expect us to walk perfectly, without stumbling or falling or making a mess. We haven't figured out that God yearns for us to live joyfully, by faith, in the reality of all that He is, in the reality of His deep unconditional love for us.

I spent decades trying to hide my imperfections from God and from others. I discovered that one of the best places to hide is in the church. For years, I played hide-and-seek with God, believing that I could camouflage the truth about myself—that I'm weak and dependent and always liable to fall—by joining another Bible study, or getting involved in another outreach ministry. I could somehow blend in with the crowd on Sundays, Tuesday mornings, and Wednesday nights. On the days and nights in between, I pretended I wasn't standing naked before the God who is everywhere present, wherever I am, at all times.

But hiding is tiresome work.

Weary, discouraged, finally I let myself ask the question that had been niggling at the back of my mind for too long: Is this all there is?

I didn't dare ask it out loud—Christians don't ask that kind of question, I thought. (I was still wearing camouflage.) Mulling in secret, I asked, is this the best I can hope for? Is this how it's going to be for me for the rest of my life—this urgent, fear-driven need to keep the rules, the constant dread of failure, the compulsion to hide so that no one finds out what a fraud I am? Could it be there's something more for me and I'm missing out?

It was the beginning of an awakening. Slowly, over time, as I grew increasingly discontent with what I thought was the walk of faith, God began to convince me that He loves me. That walking with Him doesn't mean tiptoeing through life, always afraid of tripping, afraid of toppling, afraid of being seen as one is who able to fall. It doesn't mean living on the lookout for hiding places.

The walk of faith is just that—taking one step at a time in faith, believing what He tells me: that His love is there for me. It is love that found me when I was His enemy. It won't desert me now that I'm His child.

During that time of struggling and trying to break out of the prison of legalism, I was drawn to the classic Christian writers whose passion for knowledge of God stirred me, writers whose greatest joy was found in basking in the presence of God. For months, I soaked in the writings of saints who had made God their hiding place, saints like Madame Guyon, Brother Lawrence, and Francois Fenelon. They had discovered themselves loved deeply and unconditionally. I read and reread the familiar Bible passages that taught God's love, and prayed for the truth to sink in to my soul. It was a slow, sacred journey to the place where I finally began to believe in the truth of my belovedness.

I found myself reading the Gospels with new eyes, seeing Jesus' gentleness toward humble sinners, His patience toward His disciples, His kindness and genuine pleasure in those who sought Him and wanted to know Him.

The Jesus who emerged for me was not a stoic figure who carried out an eternal plan; He was not a Savior who, seeing me as the product of His sacrifice, was less than pleased with the outcome. I began to see Him as the "Friend of sinners."

Every follower of Christ who longs to truly know God will have a unique experience with grace that plunges them into the reality of His love. He will use our weariness, our failures, catastrophes large and small, to finally force us to look at the truth of our lives: that we have never really believed what we say we believe. That we have never truly trusted what He tells us.

We can't embrace the full impact of God's ever-presence, and find comfort and joy in it, unless we begin to believe, wholeheartedly, that God loves us with an everlasting, unconditional love.

John Piper wrote, "What could God give us to enjoy that would prove Him most loving? . . . Only one possible answer: Himself. If He withholds himself from our companionship and contemplation, no matter what else He gives us, He is not loving."[3]

For me, for you, for all of God's children, there is nothing more precious, more wonderful for us than to live in the reality of His omnipresence; to live in the reality of His splendid perfection—knowing we never can be isolated from His loving gaze, never hidden from His care. If He were to withhold Himself, or barricade Himself from us, all His assurances of love and mercy would be false. All His promises would be lies. And all our hope, futile.

For us, there is no greater comfort than this: Wherever we turn, God is there.

He Knows Everything!

The priest thought there was a drunk in the temple. The woman near the altar was crying, moving her lips, probably swaying and moaning. The priest was entitled to point out her drinking problem and throw her out of the temple. But she wasn't drunk. She was in anguish, pleading with God for a child. And when God answered that prayer with a son, she went back to the temple and prayed her thanksgiving.

Hidden in that prayer is this little phrase: "Do not keep talking so proudly or let your mouth speak such arrogance, for the LORD is a God who knows, and by him deeds are weighed" (1 Samuel 2:3).

In the celebration of God's sweet gift to her, she was humbled by His omniscience. God knew all about her, about her needs, her yearnings; He knew what was best for her, best for the nation of Israel. He evaluated, considered, and granted her request based on His infinite knowledge of all things.

Hannah's prayer sums up for us all that God's omniscience means for us: He knows everything, understands everything. He is never startled or caught off guard. And His knowledge includes wisdom that discerns, makes determinations, and decides about people, events, and everything that occurs in the vast distances of His universe.

"He knows all that can be known . . . is never surprised, never amazed."[4]

This is humbling news. Hannah warned herself to be careful how she spoke to God—to remember that there was nothing she could tell Him that He didn't already know.

There are no secrets we can keep from Him. We are laid bare before His omniscience. We have nothing to boast about.

But it is good news too. Because how much help could God be to me if He was working from a deficit of information?

If God had to rely on me for a daily report before He acted in my life, or in the universe, how reliable would He be? If God needed help understanding, making decisions and weighing deeds, our universe would have long ago ceased to exist.

Solomon wrote, "By wisdom the LORD laid the earth's foundations, by understanding he set the heavens in place; by his knowledge the deeps were divided and the clouds let drop the dew" (Proverbs 3:19–20).

In Ezekiel, God basically said, "I know what is going on in your mind, Israel" (see 11:5).

And Peter, in the presence of Christ, cried, "Lord, you know all things!" (John 21:17).

In the beginning verses of Psalm 139, David acknowledged, "You know me, Lord, what I do, where I've been, when I sit and when I stand; You know all my ways and all my words, even before I speak them" (my paraphrase).

The British preacher Arthur Pink described God's omniscience like this:

> God not only knows whatsoever has happened in the
> past in every part of His vast domains, and He is not
> only thoroughly acquainted with everything that is
> now transpiring throughout the entire universe, but
> He is also perfectly cognizant of every event,
> from the least to the greatest, that ever will
> happen in the ages to come. God's knowledge
> of the future is as complete as His knowledge of
> the past and present, and that, because the future
> depends entirely upon Himself.[5]

What does this mean for me in my walk of faith?

It means He knows circumstances I'll never be privy to, events and people, present and future, who are all a part of the grand story in which I find myself, and He knows that the end is going to be glorious for His children, even if the chapter I'm living in right now is mysterious and frightening.

When chaos breaks into the quiet of my life, I can trust God, rest in His omniscience, because nothing is beyond His knowledge; no solution lies beyond His wisdom; no catastrophe ever catches Him by surprise.

God knows the full truth about me, the truth that I struggle with day after day—truth that is laid bare before the God who knows all things.

> No unsuspected weakness in our characters can come
> to light to turn God away from us, since He knew us
> utterly before we knew Him and called us to Himself
> in full knowledge of everything that was against us. . . .
> His knowledge of our afflictions and adversities . . . is
> personal, warm, and compassionate.[6]
>
> —A. W. TOZER

Nothing is hidden from God. In every tiny space of His vast universe, His knowledge penetrates, His wisdom reigns. He knows everything there is to know about everything, and that includes me. Still, He loves me.

Yes, this is humbling news. It is also great news.

The Nothing-He-Cannot-Do One

When Dick Hillis arrived in China in 1933 at twenty years old, his greatest challenge was the language. Besides being difficult to read and write, many Mandarin words are similar, so similar in sound that even the slightest mis-pronunciation can sabotage an otherwise inspired message. Once, Dick discovered that he had preached an entire sermon about a pig coming down from heaven—a slight inflection would have changed "pig" to "Lord."

Daily Dick struggled to find a way to express the person of the infinite God to a people for whom the word "god" suggested a stone-chiseled figure, or a wooden carving. How to communicate the immensity of the power and wisdom of a Being who is everywhere present at all times, with unmatched strength and perfect control of all things seen and unseen?

Dick's language teacher, Mr. Kong, supplied this idiom: "The Nothing-He-Cannot-Do One."[7]

There on the plains of Hunan, the idea of a God whose power is unlimited grabbed the imaginations of Chinese villagers. They began to see that the Christian God is unlike the stone and wooden figures they worshiped and feared and attempted to placate. Certainly, "what comes into our minds when we think about God is the most important thing about us."[8]

When crisis hits, what's the first thing that comes to your mind about God? Do you instantly think about the God of the Bible, the One you call Father, whose power knows no limits, whose strength cannot be overwhelmed by any other force? The God who has the "ability and strength whereby He can bring to pass whatsoever He please, whatsoever His infinite wisdom can direct, and whatsoever the infinite purity of His will can resolve"?[9]

The psalmist wrote, "O LORD God Almighty, who is like you? You are mighty, O LORD, and your faithfulness surrounds you. . . . Your arm is endued with power; your hand is strong, your right hand exalted" (89:8, 13).

Trace the narrative of God's omnipotence through the

book of Job. See Him claim His power over nature, over His creatures, over the heavens, over every imaginable event. Nothing lies outside His ability to control, to change, or to destroy.

He is the "Nothing-He-Cannot-Do One."

Imagine power so great that by merely speaking a word, breathing out a syllable, the heavens were made! (see Psalm 33:6, 9). And not the heavens only, but the earth too, and all its inhabitants—you and me, without ever breaking a sweat!

He made it all, exerting His incomparable power; and by that power He preserves it.

"Through Him all things were made; without him nothing was made that has been made" (John 1:3).

It is power that is at work in the farthest-flung galaxies and beyond: "He rules forever by his power"; it is power that is personal: "How awesome his works in man's behalf!" (Psalm 66:7, 5).

Tozer wrote:

> The worshiping man finds this knowledge a source of wonderful strength for his inner life. His faith rises to take the great leap upward into the fellowship of Him who can do whatever He wills to do, for whom nothing is hard or difficult because He possesses power absolute. . . . He expends no energy which must be replenished. . . . All the power required to do all that He wills to do lies in undiminished fullness in His own infinite being.[10]

All power for doing anything that needs doing in all the immeasurable distance of the universe, as well as in the smallest, most trivial details of my little life—how could we worship anyone less than omnipotent?

The theology of God's omnipotence is essential for weak, frail creatures like us. It is also at times baffling.

The Dilemma

The theology of God's omnipresence, His omniscience, combined with His omnipotence can be disturbing to even the mightiest saints.

How to sit in the presence of a friend whose child has died at the hand of a drunk driver and not wonder: Where was God's power?

If God knows all things, why did He allow this sweet child to be in that place at that time?

If God is always present, and always unlimited in His strength, why did He stand by and let this terrible thing happen when He could have prevented it?

I have prayed for broken marriages, sick friends, troubled children, and hurting churches. Sometimes God has demonstrated His power in amazing ways. Sometimes He has shed light and wisdom and given direction that couldn't be mistaken. Sometimes He hasn't.

Churches have split. Marriages have dissolved. Children have self-destructed. And I have wondered: Where was God?

A friend whose child was molested asked, "Where was His power?"

What kind of wisdom allows a child to be raped?

How are we to be comforted by a God who, for all His power and knowledge, sat still on His throne when He could have breathed a word, blinked an eye and the outcome of a life would have been different? How do we worship a God who didn't lift a finger to protect the weakest among us, those who are "the least" He said He came to save?

The dilemma of an omnipresent God who is all-powerful and all knowing is one every believer must wrestle with. And in the end, like Jacob, we must surrender to the mystery of His transcendence.

We surrender to the truth that the infinite wisdom of God will allow and direct events in our lives that will baffle us and test our trust in His goodness and love.

We surrender to the truth that God's presence is not a guarantee that bad things won't happen to us, because we live outside of Eden. We live in a place where evil wields a power too, and we cannot always escape the vile swing of its angry scythe.

The *Lord of the Rings* books and films are a powerful reminder that real evil *does* exist; that good people *do* suffer. One of my favorite scenes from the movie shows the hobbits Frodo and Sam surrounded by the desolation of a recent battle. Weary and frightened, they are overwhelmed. But Sam reminds them both that "the stories that really matter are full of darkness and light."[11]

That's a timeless truth. It was true in Galilee, when Jesus sobbed and begged, "Father, if you are willing, take this cup from me, yet not my will, but yours be done" (Luke 22:42).

It is true for us, today.

The stories that really matter—God's story, and the subplots of our smaller stories—are full of darkness and light. It is a fact we can't escape.

Wrestle with it we must. But in our wrestling, we encounter God as He really is, the Author and Finisher of this great story, a story that, in our finite experience, is not yet finished. Indeed, "the play is only in Act 3 or 4."[12]

We may argue and fuss, and cry and scream, but in the end, as agony shreds our hearts, when we have succumbed to His greater strength and wisdom, when we let ourselves sink against His heart in exhaustion, we will be forever changed.

Like Jacob, when we have wrestled with God, we will never again walk the same. Our gait will be forever altered by the power of His touch. His blessing heavy on us, our step halted, we will not hastily rush into assumptions about the nature and character of God. We will not run after other hurting souls with simplistic, trite answers for the pain that gnaws at their souls. We will walk more humbly in the shadow of His omnipotence. We will close our mouths in the presence of His omniscience, and in His presence we will bow in worship.

Questions will linger, but the vehemence behind them, the demanding hubris will be gone.

I still wonder at times why my sister Susie battles cancer.

I wonder about injured children and broken hearts.

I wonder why God withholds from me things I ask for when it is in His power to give them. Nothing stands in His way that He can't sweep aside. Nothing is too hard for Him.

The questions still come, unbidden, because I'm weak and frail and easily frightened. But I'm growing less insistent on answers. And I'm not so quick to fuss at God and demand that He perform. Because of one reason only: I'm learning to trust God.

That's the only key to rest.

It's simple, but not easy. Because we so often forget that the "Emmanuel Agenda" is different from ours.

What I want, how I want it, and when I want it doesn't always line up with what God knows is best and what will work into His perfect eternal scheme. But really believing that His wisdom and knowledge are perfect makes a difference.

Somehow, truly knowing and resting in the truth that God's power is always at work for the greatest good, for

His highest glory, and the most perfect eternal outcome alters me in a mysterious, wonderful way. In some kind of divine alchemy, holy expectation gets mixed in with my anguish, and my pain becomes not only bearable, it becomes redemptive.

Through the Rearview Mirror

"Sometimes you only understand God's power and wisdom in hindsight," Donna said.

My neighbor is sitting at home this week awaiting a hysterectomy.

Could God heal her before the surgery date? Yes, of course.

Will He? Who knows?

When God wields His power, it is not always dramatic, like fiery chariots outside the door—in fact, I've never seen a fiery chariot. I don't know anyone who has.

But I have heard the testimonies of many who said God came through for them with power and wisdom that boggled their minds.

Today, Donna is amazed. "I met an unusual woman a few months ago and God seemed to be telling me to befriend her. It was an unlikely friendship—we didn't seem to have much in common, but we began praying for one another and learning to really care about each other. Who else but this friend was working in the hospital when I went to the emergency room last week?" she told me.

"There she was, the receptionist who has firsthand information on all the doctors, which ones return patients' phone calls, which ones have the best reputation among the staff. She helped me find a doctor for a second opinion, and she was there for me with all kinds of encouragement."

Donna testifies to wisdom at work in a chance encounter with a stranger, wisdom often seen only in hindsight.

Recently, my sister Susie went to visit Erin for a day. When she walked into the house, three grandchildren swamped her. She looked around at the chores that needed doing and thought, *I really ought to do the laundry and clean house for Erin and take the kids to the park, and* . . . Then, in the next instant, she thought, *I can't! I don't have the energy for this today.*

And she really didn't.

But she recalled that when she lived there, in the earlier months after Erin's surgeries, she had found reserves of strength far beyond her own. She had all she needed to get up before dawn, make breakfast for a family of five, clean house, wash diapers, make formula, care for Erin, load toddlers into car seats to drive Erin to the doctor, or the hospital, or the radiologist. She had energy enough for fixing supper, playing with children, haggling with insurance representatives, and organizing the next day's routine of radiation treatments, preschool field trips, and grocery store runs. She had strength left over at the end of the day to read bedtime stories to a toddler and rock infant twins to sleep.

"We don't always recognize the power of God when it is working for us," Susie said, "but later we can see how He came through for us."

Philip Yancey wrote, "A person who lives in faith must proceed on incomplete evidence, trusting in advance what will only make sense in reverse."[13]

God's power and wisdom is always there for us; sometimes our best view of it is through the rearview mirror.

Hardened Hearts

Remember the night Jesus walked out to His disciples on the whitecaps of a stormy lake? I am fascinated by the "asides" in that story in Mark's gospel. Jesus, standing on shore, saw His friends struggling. He let them strain and fight with the elements when He could have come sooner, but He waited until the fourth watch and then He stepped out onto the waves and walked to them. Tucked into that account is this phrase, "He was about to pass by them" (Mark 6:48).

What? He would have walked by and not helped them?

He would have walked right on by, never revealing Himself, never letting them experience the staggering realization that He is the God of the winds and seas?

What does this mean?

Who knows? God doesn't explain this mystery, except to explain that when God is present in our catastrophes, His responses and actions sometimes will bewilder us. But there is one hint in this passage that suggests that life-altering experiences with the power of God may be limited by the condition of our hearts. Just hours earlier, those same disciples had eaten the loaves and fishes that Jesus multiplied to feed five thousand, but they had not understood. Their tummies were full, but their hearts were hardened.

There's a warning here, I think: If we are not aware and worshiping God, if our hearts are hard toward Him, we risk missing a courtside seat when the power of God goes to work for us. And even though His love and goodness compel Him to come to our aid, even though He may rescue us, if our hearts are hard, He may "pass on by." And although we find ourselves safe, unharmed, we will miss out on the life-changing knowledge that God has been at work for us. We will credit circumstances, or our own strength, or fickle weather patterns for our amazing escape, and we will miss out on an amazing experience of grace and intimacy.

Who's in Charge?

When my niece Amy was about to give birth to her third child, her oldest, five-year-old Kalyn, said, "This is just too many! I don't know how I'm going to take care of all of you!"

The whole family whooped in laughter at Kalyn's comment. It's true she's a pleasing force in her small world, but her kindergarten strength is no match for the large demands of family life. Sometimes she recognizes that; often she doesn't. And when she doesn't, it is her parents' job to remind her.

I need the same reminder. My strength is not enough for the challenges of my life.

When chaos breaks loose—in world events, in relationships, in work, in health matters—my weakness is all too obvious. I realize how much I need someone whose power is far greater than mine will ever be.

I need an omnipotent God.

This is the only kind of God who can take care of me, and you, and all of us.

I need to know that the full power of God is at work, directed and restrained, operative and active within the bounds of His perfect knowledge and wisdom. No place is hidden from Him or beyond His awesome presence.

In a world that is both darkness and light, the wisdom of God is our hope; His presence is our comfort; His power our courage.

This resurrection life you received from God is not a timid, grave-tending life. It's adventurously expectant, greeting God with a childlike, "What's next, Papa?" God's Spirit touches our spirits and confirms who we really are. We know who he is, and we know who we are: Father and children.

—ROMANS 8:15–16 THE MESSAGE

This is our identity in Christ. We are beloved children whose Father is unlimited in His power; He is present always and everywhere, and wise and all knowing. Although our world appears often to be filled only with darkness and tragedy, "it is Christ, not culture, that defines our lives. It is the help we experience, not the hazards we risk, that shapes our days."[14]

There is a profound glory in that statement. Hazards cannot always be avoided, no matter how carefully we live. But to think that our lives are not shaped so much by those hazards, which shake us to our very bones, but rather by the help we experience!

We are shaped by the power of God, by His wisdom, His presence. These are the things that make us into the people we so want to be—people of character, of compassion, of courage and contentment.

These are the things that shape us into the likeness of Christ. Never are we so vulnerable to that shaping process than when we are put in places where our weaknesses are revealed. Never are we so glad for the power and wisdom and presence of God than when we have encountered difficult times, for "we never know what strength is till our own weakness drives us to trust omnipotence; never understand how safe our refuge is till all other refuges fail us."[15]

 TRACKING GRACE

OUR LIFE IS, AT EVERY MOMENT, SUPPLIED BY HIM:
OUR TINY, MIRACULOUS POWER OF FREE WILL ONLY OPERATES
ON BODIES WHICH HIS CONTINUAL ENERGY
KEEPS IN EXISTENCE——OUR VERY POWER TO THINK
IS HIS POWER COMMUNICATED TO US.[16]

—C. S. LEWIS

Now to him who is able to do immeasurably more than
all we ask or imagine, according to his power that it is at
work within us, to him be glory in the church and in Christ
Jesus throughout all generations, for ever and ever!

—EPHESIANS 3:20–21

1. Considering God's omnipresence, are you comforted, or are you troubled?

2. What does it mean to you to know that God's wisdom is at work, directing His power?

3. Knowing that nothing is too hard for God, what pressing concern can you bring to Him in faith?

4. In what circumstances have you seen God's omni-attributes "in the rearview mirror"?

5. How might your life change if you resolved, with His help, to trust God's wisdom, rely on His power, and rest in the comfort of His presence?

GOD IS UNCHANGEABLE WITH RE-
GARD TO HIS WILL AND PURPOSE . . .
WHATSOEVER GOD HAS DECREED,
IS IMMUTABLE; WHATSOEVER GOD
HAS PROMISED, SHALL BE
ACCOMPLISHED. WHAT COMFORT
WOULD IT BE TO PRAY TO A GOD
THAT, LIKE A CHAMELEON,
CHANGED COLOURS EVERY DAY,
EVERY MOMENT?[1]

STEPHEN CHARNOCK

I the LORD do not change.
—MALACHI 3:6

CHAPTER SEVEN

Nothing's Changed— It Never Will

GOD IS IMMUTABLE

Lynnette was in turmoil. Her husband, Chuck, suffers from early-onset Alzheimer's. Until recently, Lynnette cared for him at home, but when she learned she had cancer and needed a hysterectomy, everything changed. Chuck would have to go to a live-in facility that provided full care. Just thinking about telling him was killing her.

How would she say it?

Would he understand?

They had been married nearly thirty-four years—not long enough for all their dreams to come true, but, it seemed, long enough for a nightmare to descend. In his early sixties, Chuck should have been enjoying retirement, embarking on adventures he and Lynnette had waited a lifetime to share. Instead, Lynnette was exploring Alzheimer's wings in nursing homes, alone. The agony wore on her as she tried to figure out how to tell Chuck about the changes in the coming days.

"Are you feeling down?" Chuck asked her one night as she was getting ready for bed.

Lynnette was stunned. It had been a long time since Chuck had been able to key in on her emotions, a long time since he had initiated a conversation.

"Are you asking if I'm sad?" she said.

"Yes."

Lynnette hesitated, not sure she was ready to have this painful conversation. But when Chuck asked again, she told him yes, that she had been feeling very down lately. She explained that he was going to have to go live in another place and be cared for by other people because she needed an operation.

"Why?" Chuck asked.

Lynnette hesitated again.

Chuck insisted, "Why?"

Lynnette probed him to be sure what he was really asking, and then, with resignation, she told him about the cancer.

Once again he surprised her by expressing deep sadness for her. "You shouldn't have to go through that," he said.

For the next little while, Lynnette and Chuck talked about how God had been faithful to them throughout their marriage. They talked about His promises—that He would never leave them or forsake them.

"God can't change, because He's incapable of changing," Lynnette said.

They were having a conversation—the very one Lynnette didn't know how to have. Chuck spoke without his usual difficulties—no struggle for words, no anger and frustration. He was aware, comprehending; they were communing as husband and wife for the first time in a very long time. Lynnette told me:

> By this time I had crawled into bed. We held hands, and he prayed for me, and I prayed for him. That was one of the most precious moments of our marriage, and I cannot thank God enough for allowing us this moment.
>
> I know Chuck will not remember this conversation, but the Lord allowed it for me. He knew I needed to share my heart with Chuck, and Chuck was able to share his heart with me. It was a special gift from God that I will treasure.

Lynnette and I are e-mail friends. She sent me this message a few days after she shared that story with her friends and family:

> It seems to have taken a lifetime for me to grasp some basic truths about God, but one of the most precious and [strengthening] things to me is the immutability of God. He cannot be anything other than who He is, because He is God and cannot change. . . . I can no longer be with Chuck and take care of him as before, but the same God who lives in me, lives in him. What a connection!

Lynnette's e-mail sent me on a treasure hunt for the significance of God's immutability. Digging into Bible passages, I found myself standing in awe of the God whose attributes never change, who can neither increase, nor decrease; whose goodness and love are always immense and extravagant. But His immutability is so much more than a theological statement assuring us that God won't one day morph into a being we don't recognize.

Bursting out of the Scriptures was the picture of the God whose essence is found in His eternal, never-changing passion for three things: communion, holiness, and glory.

For these three, the Son gave His life.

The Power of Words

Lynnette's moment of joy coincided with communion.

Words shared, understood, received, responded to. Such a simple thing: talking and being heard.

Such a profound thing.

Every syllable we shape, every sound we utter is a metaphor of heaven's eloquence.

> *By the word of the LORD were the heavens made,*
> *their starry host by the breath of his mouth. . . .*
> *He spoke, and it came to be;*
> *he commanded, and it stood firm.*
> —PSALM 33:6, 9

A puff of breath, a sound formed, a planet appears.

Mountains erupt, rivers tumble. Creatures lumber and crawl and gallop and slither and climb and fly and swim— all in response to the words spoken by God.

> *The voice of the LORD is over the waters . . .*
> *The voice of the LORD is powerful;*
> *the voice of the LORD is majestic. . .*
> *The voice of the LORD strikes with flashes of lightning.*
> *The voice of the LORD shakes the desert.*
> —PSALM 29:3–8

Conversation fills the cosmos as the Trinity communes in creation.

The Father, Son, and Holy Spirit, exulting in the splendor and beauty of holiness, exist eternally in fellowship, in relationship, in communion with each other—with *voices*, with *words*, with *conversation.*

For me, a word person, this is an amazing thing to think about. I grew up in a household where conversation was valued, almost revered.

I grew up believing that conversation is essential to relationship, that when two people engage in conversation, there is the chance for connection. Without it, there is none.

This isn't a news flash, really. We all know this, on some level. Communication is so vital, so essential to us that we are constantly trying to improve it. Stroll the self-help aisles of your neighborhood bookstore. Count the titles that address communication skills. Why so much effort at figuring out how to make it work? Because we know that without it, there can be no relationship, and no true communion. Without it, there can be no hope of joy.

Recently, I sat on a panel to discuss Christians and the arts and culture. On my left was a seminary professor with two earned doctorates. Next to him was a talented young man with an advanced degree in art. He paints, owns a local gallery, and travels extensively to buy and sell art. I was in over my head, and I knew it, but the invitation to join them was irresistible. I wasn't thrilled about being in front of an audience for the actual discussion, but I was excited about getting together, just the three of us, to plan the workshop and explore the topic.

We met at a Starbucks—the professor, the artist, and the writer. We jousted, sparred, came at each other with probing questions and, at times, challenged each other's insights. I had planned to just listen—what could I contribute, really? But the conversation pulled me in. I couldn't sit in silence. I had to participate.

Two people I had never met became known to me in those two short encounters. Through conversation, we shared our passion for art, for literature; we talked about journalistic ethics, about Christians and creativity. We shared excitement and a common challenge to express the truth of God with excellence; to probe the limits of our imaginations to produce work that expresses the transcendent nature of the God of all creation. And brief though it was, and probably never to be repeated, it was an experience of great communion.

Now, just imagine—being in conversation with God —this is the God whose name Israel feared to speak aloud. He invites us into conversation with Him! He approaches us through the living Word, initiates relationship with us, and then settles into a life of communion with us that will never end.

We Ought to Listen

God has always been about conversation—within the Trinity, in eternity past, discussing Creation: "Let us make man in our image" (Genesis 1:26).

God has always been about communicating with His creation to alert them to His presence, His grandeur, His character, His plan for the redeemed—and the rebellious.

In the garden, He talked with Adam and Eve. He called out to them, even when they were in hiding.

Scan the pages of your Bible. Listen to God speak to people.

To Abraham: "Follow me to a land that you don't know."

To Moses: "Lead my people out of Egypt."

To a sleeping child: "Samuel, Samuel," and when he's wide awake, "I am about to do something in Israel that will astonish everyone in the land."

To a cupbearer: "Go build Me a wall."

To shepherds, kings, washed-up kings, generals, wine-press operators, and prophets—God spoke words they could hear, words they could pass on to others. Words that condemned, words that anointed, words that instructed, words that revealed, words that mystified, words that startled and thrilled. But always, always, God spoke, even when His voice wasn't welcome.

The Israelites hovered in terror when they saw thunder and lightning and smoke on the mountain where Moses was meeting with God. They heard the roar, felt the earth tremble, and were scared silly. "Moses, you tell us what God has to say," they begged, "but don't have Him talk to us directly or we'll die!" (Exodus 20:19, my paraphrase).

Imagine! Our God in heaven is so grand, so awesome, that His speech can stir up billows of smoke. It can shake the ground and light up the sky and rumble like thunder in a summer storm, or it can whisper in a still small voice.

It is the Word.

The Word of God, fleshed out for us by the incarnate Son, will never be silenced. It will never change. As the psalmist writes, "Your word, O LORD, is eternal; it stands firm in the heavens" (119:89).

And the Word, our Lord, says of Himself: "Heaven and earth will pass away, but my words will never pass away" (Mark 13:31).

Beyond Trifles

Maybe you're reading this and you're thinking, if God is the eternal Word, why do I sometimes feel like He's talking to everyone but me?

Am I the only one who has ever felt as though God were giving me the silent treatment?

Why am I unable to hear His voice?

There are times for all of us when no matter how hard we may listen, we cannot hear Him. There are times when, above our groaning and sobbing, all we can hear is the shattering of a breaking heart.

Madame Guyon wrote, "You *will* have dry times."[2] Certainly there will be silent times—times you have to fight through if you're going to hear from God.

These are the times John Piper had in mind when he wrote, "No one ever said that they learned their deepest lessons of life, or had their sweetest encounters with God, on the sunny days. People go deep with God when the drought comes. That is the way God designed it."[3]

Drought hits, and trivia gags us.

We don't have time for trifles. We listen for God with greater intensity, more focused attention. If our ears cannot hear, our eyes must find His words on the written page, and there we anchor ourselves in truth. We grab hold, by faith, sometimes with sweat-slick hands, but we hang on. We don't let go of the truth.

In those moments, when it seems as though God refuses to speak, sheer trust is all we have. It's the gut-wrenching kind, the kind that, against all odds, refuses to stop believing that God is present, that He is good, that He is faithful. In spite of silence, the soul that believes that it is loved keeps on listening, keeps on going to God, reading His words, expecting that, in a moment of sudden relief, a resonance will be felt, like a vibration in the soul, even if the sounds of the syllables can't be distinguished.

Finally, God's voice breaks through. We find ourselves spoken to. And the conversation deepens, because God isn't content with trivia either. He takes us to places in our souls we've never visited, addressing life matters we never before wanted to explore—things like true worship and abandonment to God. We can't escape the questions we dodged during easier times; questions like: Do you love Me, or Do you love your comfortable life?

Do you trust Me? Do you treasure Me?

Do you believe that I love you dearly?

Sometimes His voice will echo in our hearts, mystifying and mesmerizing us: "My sheep listen to my voice; I know them, and they follow me" (John 10:27).

Often, He will speak peace and comfort to us through the mouths of His people who share with us the same sweet messages God whispered to them when they were hurting.

Most of the time, it will be the truth of His written Word that etches itself on our souls, and we "listen" not with our ears, but with our eyes glued to the page, our whole conscious being engaged in discerning what God has to say to us.

Trust surges. Faith grows. God becomes more real to us because His words have found a home in our souls.

Intimacy deepens, because God Almighty, through the Eternal Word, has communed with us.

God always has been about relationship. Before He formed the world, He was set on bringing sons and daughters into His family (Ephesians 1:4–5). He invites us in with words. He brings us in through the Word made flesh.

Relationship occurs. Communion happens. Joy erupts.

This is the unchanging message of the Trinity. This is the story told at the manger in Bethlehem; this is the story

Jesus told as He shared His life with the disciples. This is the story He told on the cross, gasping, bleeding, dying. This is the story that brightened the empty tomb when the angels arrived, their words lighting the darkness like a heavenly marquee: "See! This is the length to which God will go to have a relationship with you! Don't settle for anything less!"

To those who hear and heed the message, God will give them "dazzling illuminations and convert them into heroes."[4]

Heroes of faith, like Lynnette and Chuck.

With and for Us

I'd like to be a hero too. But I confess, I'm more often cowardly.

I'm a middle child, non-confrontational, compliant, more anxious to make peace than war.

Sometimes I'm unsure about the things that need fighting for, or against. Mostly, I just don't want to have to fight at all.

For much of my life of faith, I struggled to keep the image of Jesus the Lamb front and center in my theology. The grip of legalism made the image of a lion too frightening. I might, on a good day, be able to imagine cuddling up to the gentle warmth of a lamb, but the idea of curling up next to the Lion of Judah terrified me.

It took years for God to convince me that I am loved, that I am safe in His presence not only because of the blood of the Lamb, but also because of the ferocity of the Lion who fights for my holiness every day, every hour of every day.

The immutable God who calls us into communion through the Word is also the eternal King of Kings who began the battle against the Enemy of our souls before God sank the steel and piers for the foundation of this earth (see Ezekiel 28:14–15).

The battle, for our souls, for our purity and sanctity, rages still. And the eternal, unchanging Christ we call our Lover and Friend fights for us, and with us.

Our holiness is His consuming passion.

Why do we so often forget this?

When chaos breaks into our lives, when despair and hopelessness threaten, when temptation rages wild and terrifying, the Lion of Judah roars across the horizon, challenging the enemies of our souls to battle. His strength and ferocity are unmatched by any force known to man or demon. But, like the children of Israel who let the fear of giants in the land paralyze them, we panic.

It's a great old story, a timeless story.

A report of danger ahead hits camp, and Israel balks, too afraid to keep going forward in the journey.

It didn't matter that God had called them out of Egypt and named them His unique, holy people, set apart for a special relationship, a special destiny.

It didn't matter that He had been with them every step of the way for years—a cloud they could follow by day and a pillar of fire that lit the darkness and gave warmth at night and discouraged marauding bandits. It didn't matter that He had been providing breakfast every morning, a kind of divine carry-out service, and they had no worries about shopping, or planting, or harvesting. They just opened the tent flap, picked up the groceries delivered overnight, and then set out to follow wherever God led them.

Until they got word of giants ahead.

And not only giants, but large walled cities and savage tribes. Suddenly, the journey wasn't so appealing.

But God reassured them, saying, "Do not be terrified; do not be afraid of them. The LORD your God, who is going before you, will fight for you, as he did for you in Egypt, before your very eyes, and in the desert. There you saw how the LORD your God carried you, as a father carries his son, all the way you went until you reached this place" (Deuteronomy 1:29–31).

But the people were too afraid.

Nothing God said convinced them that He would be faithful to His promises. It seemed nothing He said and nothing He had done in the past warranted their trust.

It's easy to point fingers at the nation of Israel, but my own everyday scenario isn't much different. Is yours?

Every day we awaken to the omnipresent God who has given us life and every good and perfect gift. Every day we eat His provision; we breathe because His sovereign goodness and mercy give us air and lungs. We walk out into the adventure of life because His omnipotence energizes us and sustains us.

And then, one day, giants appear. The company we work for is considering downsizing. A mammogram shows something suspicious. We learn a family member is ill, or in trouble. Whatever the case, we find ourselves overwhelmed. The route ahead looks dangerous, and we don't want to make the journey. Our faith falters.

We no longer see ourselves as God's holy people, uniquely set apart to live in the joy of His love; we no longer view ourselves as ones chosen and established in a relationship unlike all other relationships. We may have been branded by God's very own hand, but we are too troubled to see it. We are wringing our hands with worry instead of tracing His mark on our souls.

Suddenly, in the face of giants, we think ourselves

victims instead of victors. Horror is our obsession; holiness is vague and impossibly distant.

God's message is the same for us today, as it was for Israel: "You are mine, and I will fight for you. Don't be afraid."

But we aren't convinced. In spite of all He has done for us in the past, along the way, we aren't convinced He is big enough to take care of us if we find ourselves in the presence of giants.

We aren't convinced God can be trusted—this time.

We aren't convinced He will come through for us—this time.

Because we have forgotten that we are His.

We have forgotten, or refused to believe, the truth about the God of Israel. He is the same Lion-King who fought for the people He chose as His own, who went to war to maintain their identity, to protect their unique status as His own, to ensure their possession of the Promised Land.

We have forgotten that the God who fought for the sanctity and holiness of His people Israel has sworn to do the same for us. We belong to Him. His brand seared our souls, and we can never be claimed by another. Our eternal fate sealed by His Spirit, holiness is our destiny.

Because holiness, our distinct "set-apartness" as His unique people, engaged in relationship with Him, is His passion.

That will never change.

Keeping Silent

Madame Guyon, imprisoned in the Bastille for her passionate faith, wrote to a friend, "You and I are weak. At our best we are *very* weak. If you, in your weakness, attempt to attack your enemies, you will often find yourself wounded. Just as frequently, you will even find yourself defeated. There is another way. . . . Remain in faith in the simple presence of Jesus Christ. You will find an immediate supply of strength. . . . 'The Lord shall fight for you while you keep silent.'"5

It's often the "keeping silent" that is hard for us, isn't it? It was hard for Israel. They did what you and I do when we are scared and hurting, and faithless. They grumbled (see Deuteronomy 1:27–28).

They slandered God.

I've done that. I've doubted His goodness and questioned His love. I've heard God say, "Remember what I've done for you in the past, Jan. Remember what your eyes have seen, what your heart has understood. Remember who you are—you are Mine! Trust Me."

And still, I've wanted to turn somewhere else for comfort, or for safety. I've wanted to stop this trek into holiness, this journey into the heart of God, because I've begun to doubt His character. How dare He let this awful thing happen to me? How dare He bring me to this place of danger?

When finally, desperate, I remember that there is no one else to turn to, no one else who has the words of life. I close my mouth, and I learn the truth of the prophet's words, that "in quietness and trust is your strength" (Isaiah 30:15).

I hear God say, "I AM." Not, I *Was*, or I *Will Be*, or I *Might Be*.

All that He ever was, He always will be.

Always He will be committed to a relationship with me, because He chose me and marked me as His own.

Always He will be committed to communing with me, because the Word can never be silenced. The Word will never withdraw from me. His joy is the joy of fellowship and conversation.

Now, today, as always, forever, God is the same.

He is my Warrior-King, the One who fights with me, and for me, for my destiny: for holiness.

Our Warrior-King

God doesn't change. He "does not change like shifting shadows" (James 1:17).

When giants appear, in any form, it is the time to remember that our immutable God is and always will be our Warrior-King, committed to defending us, protecting us, and leading us to victory. He is and always will be committed to our holiness.

It doesn't mean we won't have to engage in fierce fighting—our most ferocious enemies will be spiritual: bitterness, rebellion, hatred, fear. Our best course of action will be to follow Madame Guyon's example—to be quiet, to listen, to trust God to fight for us, in us, to defeat the enemies of our souls. To fight for our purity and holiness.

It doesn't mean we won't feel pain and sorrow and the very literal exhaustion of battle fatigue. But it does mean that our King will fight with us, and that He will give us the ultimate victory.

The giants *will* be slain.

Satan and his minions *will* get their just deserts for the horrors they brought to this planet.

God never will accept evil; He never will acquiesce to its presence in His universe. He forever will be the Warrior-King who "maintains his wrath against his enemies. . . . The LORD will not leave the guilty unpunished" (Nahum 1:2–3).

One day Jesus will ride from heaven on a white horse

with an army behind Him and take on Satan once again. In one great battle to end all battles, He will mop up what remains of sin on the earth. He will roust the guerrilla troops who refused to surrender at the empty tomb. The scene will be too vivid for the squeamish—blood will drip from Jesus' robes, John said. "He treads the winepress of the fury of the wrath of God Almighty," and everyone will know that He is the "KING OF KINGS AND LORD OF LORDS" (Revelation 19:15, 16).

When the final battle has been fought, Jesus our King will enter heaven's halls wearing the scars that won the war. Even on that day, when the fighting is over, when the armor has been hung in the great museum hall of heaven, God will not be finished despising sin. He never will change His mind about His enemy.

When we bow in Jesus' presence, when we dance in His great halls, when we sit and commune with Him, listening to His stories, we will see the places where the nails ripped His flesh; we will see where the crown of thorns tore His forehead. And we will be reminded, forever, always, that He went to war for us, that His ferocity saved us.

He rescued us in His fierceness, because our holiness is His passion.

Our God is a Warrior-King with the heart of a lion. He gave His life to bring us the eternal joy shared by the Trinity: the joy of communion and holiness.

And to introduce us to the joy of undiminished and undiminishing glory.

When Glory Happens

Glory is a cheap commodity these days.
Or what passes for glory.

For the price of humiliation, you can go on television, sing off-key, and be skewered and slashed by a critic. In front of millions of viewers, you can be rejected by a bachelor, or bachelorette, be defeated by your worst fear, be fired from a job, and let an entire nation point and snicker at your worst physical features in hopes that you'll be chosen for an "extreme makeover."

We'll sell our dignity, barter our pride, and expose ourselves to ridicule and outlandish situations, all for a dollop of glory, or what we think of as glory in our wacky culture.

It's obvious, we're pretty confused about what real glory is. But we do have one thing right: Real glory only happens when we're in proximity to another person, in relationship. But we've gotten the "someone" all wrong. It isn't the audience on the other side of the television camera. It isn't the crowds at the football stadium, or the masses found in a media venue. It's not people at the office, members of our family, our neighbors, or our friends.

To experience real glory, you don't have to be smart or beautiful or visible to millions on a small screen.

You don't have to be fast or strong or skilled or witty or well-spoken or well-liked.

You don't have to be philanthropic or photogenic to capture glory.

Glory captures you.

God, through Christ, enters our world and captivates us with the sweet allure of His indescribable magnificence.

"The Word became flesh and made his dwelling among us," wrote John. "We have seen his glory, the glory of the One and Only, who came from the Father, full of grace and truth" (John 1:14).

Decades later, although old and frail and awaiting death in exile on Patmos, John seemed to be reminiscing with awe. "We saw with our eyes!" he told us. "We touched Him, this One and Only! We experienced His glory for ourselves!" (see 1 John 1:1).

What did it feel like, John? I'd like to ask. And I think he would fumble for words and then finally have to say it's like being drawn into a mystery so big it dwarfs you and grabs your imagination and lifts your heart and buoys your spirit until you can't even remember what boredom is. You're no longer just going through the motions of act three or four in your little personal drama; you're no longer living in anticipation of that surge of adrenaline released at the sound of human applause. You couldn't care less about applause. And this is John speaking, one of the "Sons of Thunder," (Mark 3:17) remember? He was one of the disciples who had hopes of bagging some glory for himself, expecting Jesus to rout the Romans and establish a kingdom of His own. John's mother asked Jesus to make a place of special honor for her son in that new kingdom, but I wonder if he put her up to it. I wonder if he thought Jesus wouldn't say no to his mother.

John was old when he wrote Revelation, and he understood that true glory had nothing to do with human status or performance, with social rank or physical appearance. He'd heard Jesus pray, "Father, I want those you have given me to be with me where I am, and to see my glory, the glory you have given me because you loved me before the creation of the world" (John 17:24).

It is eternal, unfading glory derived from love that is eternal, unchanging.

We experience it by being in God's presence.

And nothing drives us into His presence like suffering.

Loosened from Earth

It's a theological fact: For us, in this life, glory will be inextricably bound to suffering.

In 1663, a preacher named Thomas Watson was tossed out of his church. He believed the Bible was true, through and through, and the Church of England didn't. He wouldn't change his sermons, so the church's hierarchy sent him packing. Saddened, but not broken, he became a student of both suffering and glory. He wrote:

> Afflictions work for good, as they are the means of
> loosening our hearts from the world. When you dig
> away the earth from the root of a tree, it is to loosen
> the tree from the earth; so God digs away our earthly
> comforts to loosen our hearts from the earth.[6]

Loosened from the earth, we are carried closer to the heart of God.

God is treating us "like friends," Fenelon wrote, when He sends us "crosses, sufferings, and humiliations," using them to "draw souls to himself."[7]

And in these things, we learn to recognize genuine glory.

In close proximity to God, we experience what no other relationship can give us. We enter the mystery that is the fellowship of the Trinity. It's no use trying to describe it—any description falls short. It's like trying to describe the taste of chocolate to someone who has never had it; like trying to describe the color lavender to someone who's been blind since birth; like trying to describe the sound of Beethoven's "Adagio" from *Sonata Pathetique* to a deaf child.

Glory cannot be described in words adequate to its

experience. But this much is true: When God allows us to have a taste of it here and now, a small sampling of it, the wonder of it never leaves you. And anything less, called by the same name, is forever exposed as fake.

Glory is our destiny—life in full proximity to God, nothing between. The presence of sin eradicated, tears wiped away, all desire for our own celebrity status, our own fame and imitation glory, will be forgotten forever. We will live with God, fully aware of all that He is, exulting in His beauty.

The mystery and romance of it staggers me—this is our destiny! Living in perfect intimacy with God and enjoying Him fully, forever.

And we'll be satisfied.

Think of it: The yearning for something more, something else, or *someone* else, to make us feel complete will be quieted. The urgent cravings that stalk us will be stilled. Our restless souls will be content.

C. S. Lewis wrote, "Glory means good report with God, acceptance by God, response, acknowledgment, and welcome into the heart of things. The door on which we have been knocking all our lives will open at last."[8]

In heaven, in the presence of God, our Savior, in whom all things are held together, we will know that we are finally in that place we spent a lifetime looking for, the place we always yearned to be; we truly, finally, will be forever, "in the heart of [all] things."

This Same Jesus

It is an incredible experience to study Jesus' actions after His resurrection. To see Him show up among the disciples and convince them that, yes, it's really Jesus!

And to see Him with Thomas, saying, "Go ahead,

touch My wounds, feel My flesh—see! I'm really here!"
(See John 20:27.)

In the garden with Mary, His appearance blurred by the
tears in her eyes, or the darkness of her despair, He speaks
her name in His familiar voice, and she worships Him.

On the seaside He hunkers before a fire, cooking
breakfast for the disciples. He's the same! He loves their
company! He delights in serving them.

On the mountain He says His good-byes and the disciples stand, rubbernecking, staring up at the sky as He is lost
in the clouds. Hear the angels say, "This *same* Jesus, who has
been taken from you into heaven, will come back in the same
way you have seen him go into heaven" (Acts 1:11, italics
added).

It is this same Jesus who Lynnette clings to today.

It is this same Jesus who reaches for our hand too.

It is this same Jesus who speaks to us.

When other voices are silenced by death or distance,
when angry, accusing voices assault us, the Word, Christ
Himself, keeps speaking the words we most need to hear:
"You are mine, and if you'll let me, I'll be to you everything you need; more than you ever imagined, and could
never begin to imagine."

When our lives are filled with conflict and chaos, when
it seems everything we value is at risk, this same Jesus is
there for us. If what we have needs protecting, nothing can
stand against the fierceness of the Lion of Judah; if what
we treasure really needs defending, the vigilance of our
Warrior-King will guarantee its safety. He will fight for
us, for our purity, for our holiness, and defeat our enemies.

This same Jesus will never be content with anything
less for us than our perfect union with Him. He will chase
us relentlessly until we join Him in heaven and share His
glory. Nothing will ever deter Him from pursuing the

destiny for which He created us. He has promised Himself to us for eternity, and He will let nothing interfere with the perfect communion His love has planned.

"Jesus Christ is the same yesterday and today and forever" (Hebrews 13:8). He is the Savior who "by the power of God, who has saved us and called us to a holy life—not because of anything we have done but because of *his own purpose* and grace" (2 Timothy 1:9, italics added).

His words ring true and clear today for us as they did for ancient Israel:

> *Fear not, for I have redeemed you;*
> *I have summoned you by name; you are mine.*
> *When you pass through the waters, I will be with you;*
> *and when you pass through the rivers,*
> *they will not sweep over you.*
> *When you walk through the fire, you will not be burned;*
> *the flames will not set you ablaze.*
> *For I am the LORD, your God, the Holy One of Israel, your Savior. . . .*
> *Do not be afraid, for I am with you.*
> —ISAIAH 43:1–3, 5

Today, His promises, His protection, His purposes remain the same.

When the world's violence and terror play out in front of our eyes on the evening news, God speaks above the furor: "Don't be afraid, I am with you."

When the pathology report comes back malignant, when the bank starts foreclosure proceedings, when the divorce papers arrive, when the child we love runs away from rehab: "I am with you. Don't be afraid."

When Lynnette walks the curling linoleum floors of an Alzheimer's wing: "I am with you. Don't be afraid."

Communing with us in holy conversation, with gentleness and truth, God gives us the living Word, full of hope, full of comfort, full of assurance of His mighty wisdom and power.

Fighting for us, fighting with us, He gives us courage to trust, energy to battle despair, because He is our Warrior-King.

He pulls us close against His heart where we feel the pounding of His love, and we know, because of the death of Christ, we are accepted. We are welcomed with joy.

We are destined for glory that will never fade.

Full Circle

God's passion for communion, for holiness, for glory is all consuming and never changing. In the final moments of earth's temporal history, it will all come together as Jesus, blazing and glorious, bursts out of heaven's gate and lights up the sky with His army of angels.

The Warrior-King, the Eternal Word, will arrive to make right all wrongs. In the same way He spoke creation into existence, He will speak words that, like a sword, will "strike down the nations" that refused to follow Him (see Revelation 19:11–21).

All the enemies of God, and of His holy people, will be killed with "the sword that came out of the mouth of the rider on the horse."

The Word incarnate will *speak* and the fate of the world will be settled. He will *speak,* and the battle for holiness will be finally, forever, finished. He will speak, and communion within the family of God will be forever, finally perfected.

The Word, made flesh, will once more dwell among us. A loud voice from the throne will say: "Now the dwelling of God is with men, and he will live with them. They will be his people, and God himself will be with them and be their God. He will wipe every tear from their eyes. There will be no more death or mourning or crying or pain, for the old order of things has passed away" (Revelation 21:3–4).

Once again, He will come to us, the incarnate Word. To live with us. To commune with us.

Like men and women of centuries past, we will behold His glory, the glory of the begotten of the Father, full of grace and truth.

For this, the Son gave His life: for communion, for holiness, for glory.

This is the truth that boggles our minds. That the eternal, infinite Trinity was not content to dwell in communion and holiness and glory that would exclude us. Are you able to imagine the height and depth and length and breadth of it?

Think of it: God, self-sufficient in His immutable nature, needing nothing and no one; yet He created in His own nature a yearning for *us,* a yearning to bring *us* into the perfect circle of Trinitarian joy, making it possible for *us* to be a source of pleasure to *Him*. The thought of it should drop us to our knees. It should throw us onto our faces in humble worship and adoration.

It should conquer our souls with love.

"To please God . . . to be a real ingredient in the divine happiness . . . to be loved by God, not merely pitied, but delighted in as an artist delights in his work or a father in a son—it seems impossible, a weight or burden of glory which our thoughts can hardly sustain. But so it is."[9]

This is what God always has had in mind.

Nothing's changed. It never will.

TRACKING GRACE

NOTHING THAT HAS OCCURRED OR WILL OCCUR IN
HEAVEN OR EARTH OR HELL CAN CHANGE THE TENDER
MERCIES OF OUR GOD. FOREVER HIS MERCY STANDS, A
BOUNDLESS, OVERWHELMING IMMENSITY OF DIVINE PITY
AND COMPASSION.[10]

—A. W. TOZER

*Jesus Christ is the same yesterday
and today and forever.*
—HEBREWS 13:8

1. How does it comfort you to know that God
   never changes?

2. How would you have to correct your view
   of God to be able to find comfort in His
   immutability?

3. What does it mean to you to know that God's
   plan for you always has included communion
   and fellowship with Him?

4. What are some mistaken ideas you have held about glory?

5. Under what circumstances have you recognized Christ as your Warrior-King?

6. How are you comforted to know that God will fight for you?

7. Thinking of Christ's return, and that the victory declared by His Word shall come to pass, what is your response to the truth fact that He wants you to know His Word now?

For Christians, the source
of true joy is submitting
ungrudgingly to the
sovereign Lord we belong
to. As we abandon our-
selves to him, he gives us
an unpredictable,
extraordinary life.[1]

Brenda Waggoner

But you, O Sovereign Lord, deal well with me for
your name's sake; out of the goodness of your love,
deliver me.

—Psalm 109:21

CHAPTER EIGHT

Between the Paws of
the True Lion
GOD'S SOVEREIGNTY

"Nothing catches God by surprise, you know. He's in control of everything that happens."

I said the words with the nonchalance of one who had lived with this piece of theology comfortably, if distantly, for years, somewhat like a landlord who tolerates the presence of a benign boarder in a room above the garage.

"Whoa now! Wait just a minute!" my guest said.

She had come into my kitchen and hoisted herself up onto my countertop. There she sat, swinging her legs, her scruffy cowboy boots banging against the lower cabinets, digging gouges into my nicely stained woodwork.

I tried not to cringe. Handing her a tall iced tea, I invited her to join me at the table. She whipped herself off the counter and loped to the kitchen nook where she dropped into a chair.

"You're saying God is in control of *everything*?" She

shook her head and grinned as though I had just told her a weird, unfunny joke. "Naw, I can't believe that."

I doubted she believed anything I considered orthodox, that *any* well-schooled Christian considered orthodox. She was new to faith. Her life had been hard, harder than she was willing to tell. I tried to get her to open up with me, but she said, "You don't want to know, and I don't want to talk about it."

The women's minister at my church had encouraged me to befriend this young woman. That day, in my kitchen, was our first and only visit. She disappeared from church, from town a few weeks later, and I never heard from her again. I was relieved. The weight of her pathos bowed me. I felt threatened by the shards of her brokenness.

Although she never told me her story, her gestures and facial expressions revealed the chapter titles—abuse, rejection, cruelty, and finally, shame. Her body language told me she was a living tome of anguish. And what I had said to her, in essence, was that God could have prevented it, protected her, but He didn't.

No wonder she left as quietly as she came.

There is something about the theology of God's sovereignty that terrifies and infuriates at first acquaintance. It seems to dress God in the attire of a school yard bully who, because He's bigger and stronger and tougher than anyone else, has the right to dictate all the games, and their outcome. He chooses the teams, referees the plays, and stands by, arms folded, while His thugs beat up on those unable to defend themselves. He's too ferocious to challenge, too fast to escape. He's ever-present; His threat always palpable, sending terror into the farthest corners of the playground.

I wish I could find her again, that young woman. I wish for a "do over." This time, I would invite her onto the back porch where we would sit and rock and sip a cool drink. I would know it is more important to listen than to talk, more important to love than to educate.

I would know too, what it feels like to have walked through flames with the knowlege that someone stood nearby holding a water hose that could have quenched the fire and saved me from being scorched. Someone who *could* have. Someone who *didn't*.

The Dilemma of Sovereignty

This is the great dilemma of the theology of sovereignty.

I am God, and there is no other; I am God, and there is none like me. I make known the end from the beginning, from ancient times, what is still to come. I say: My purpose will stand, and I will do all that I please. From the east I summon a bird of prey; from a far-off land, a man to fulfill my purpose. What I have said, that will I bring about; what I have planned, that will I do.
—ISAIAH 46:9–11

His dominion is an eternal dominion; his kingdom endures from generation to generation. All the peoples of the earth are regarded as nothing. He does as he pleases with the powers of heaven and the peoples of the earth. No one can hold back his hand or say to him: "What have you done?"
—DANIEL 4:34–35

Our God is in heaven; he does whatever pleases him.
—PSALM 115:3

Are not two sparrows sold for a penny? Yet not one of them will fall to the ground apart from the will of your Father.
—MATTHEW 10:29

I will have mercy on whom I have mercy, and I will have compassion on whom I have compassion.
—ROMANS 9:15

All of us, at some time, must confront this truth: God is in charge. He's the boss. Nothing happens without Him; nothing overrules Him; nothing overpowers Him. He isn't overwhelmed or undone by anything. He sees, allows, instigates, and intervenes when he chooses. Nothing catches Him by surprise.

It is theology that will either chase us out of town, or set us dancing.

Mindful All Along

Mary stayed in town. And she's dancing.

You'd never suspect she's a survivor of sexual abuse. She wasn't much more than a toddler when she figured out she was unloved and unprotected, fatherless. When she was fifteen, she discovered the heavenly Father. She began learning about Him, experiencing Him, walking with Him by faith. When the journey led through the badlands of His sovereignty, the truth of it did not always set easy with her.

Questions tumbled, at times irate, at times humble.

"Why, God? Why let a little girl be subjected to so much pain?"

A reasonable question.

God, if You're in control of everything, if nothing happens outside Your knowledge and control, if You make the decisions and rule the universe, why do such terrible things happen?

I've asked this question, haven't you?

Why the divorce? Why the cancer diagnosis? Why the pink slip in my pay envelope last Friday?

Why the news of another child being molested?

Why this miscarriage?

Why this infertility, Lord, when we want so much to be parents?

If You are in charge of the decisions of the universe, would it be so hard, just once, to decide in my favor? Would it be so hard to choose something nice, something easy and pleasant for me?

Mary agonized. But she continued to walk, one step at a time, sometimes trudging, sometimes barely able to see where to put her foot, but always holding on to Jesus' hand, not turning back. Not running away from Him.

It was an uphill climb, as the walk of faith always is. Along the way she learned to sit and rest with Jesus; she learned to venture into the dangerous places, the places where it looks like the ground is going to drop off under your feet, but the sign promising a "scenic view" still lures you there—if you're brave enough to go.

Mary stepped out there, into the scary places. She stood on the precipice, and with Jesus holding her tight, she gazed out at the terrain of her life and saw that all the barren places, all the terrifying passages, had all led to *this* place: this place where she could feel the arms of God around her, where she could hear His voice. And all the violent twists along the path, all the fog-blurred, confusing miles she had traveled seemed suddenly, somehow, worth it.

Because they led her into the arms of God.

There, nestled close against His chest, Mary heard God singing over her. She heard the rhythms of grace in His heartbeat, and her feet were set to dancing.

And when she speaks and writes, it sounds like music, the melody rich with the blending of both major and minor chords:

At times I've wondered why God let me be born into a home of abandonment, where I was unprotected from sexual abuse. But as I travel with Jesus, I see more and more that this background has now become a dancing stage where I can dance God's healing to a world in desperate need of it. God knew it all along. He knew He would rescue me at fifteen, giving me His life for my tattered one. He knew that He could take a weakling like me and show His strength to those whose glory is their own strength. God knows it all—from my birth to today, and He will use it to glorify Himself today and in heaven. I long to live for that day when wrongs will be righted and God will wipe away my tears.

Can you hear the grace notes in her song? Can you hear its harmony with a song sung by another Mary?

My soul glorifies the Lord and my spirit rejoices in God my Savior, for he has been mindful of the humble state of his servant. . . . The Mighty One has done great things for me—holy is his name. . . . He has performed mighty deeds with his arm . . . he has filled the hungry with good things.
—LUKE 1:46–53

There is only one answer to the questions that sovereignty prompt. And it is this: God is mindful of our humiliation.

In the huge narrative that is the gospel, written before the foundation of the world by the One who is the author and finisher of our faith, God is mindful of us. He is aware of our stumbling, bumbling faith. He is aware of the horrors that haunt us and the devastation that has ripped us. He is aware and operating in His sovereign rule with divine intent—intent to redeem.

The choices He makes as our sovereign King—to act, or remain still and silent; to prevent, or not; to cure, or not —all His decisions are made with our scars and sufferings and our creaturely weaknesses in mind.

C. S. Lewis wrote that God "has paid us the intolerable compliment of loving us, in the deepest, most tragic, most inexorable sense."[2]

Nothing He does in this universe is cut off from His love, His mindfulness of who we are, what we are, what He has destined us to become. The compliment of it overwhelms us. He considers our frame, our fragile selves. He knows how easily we break, and so He wraps us in love and brings us into His family and writes our lives into the Great Story, with all its tragic twists and turns. As the plot unfolds, He is never unaware of our part in it. He never forgets us. He knows our confusion and fear. It is always taken into account, with love—deep, deep love.

This is the answer to God's disturbing sovereignty. The question it begs is this: Will we let that be enough for us?

Will God Be Enough?

This is really the question that haunts our living, every day, every hour, in this life that is filled with catastrophes, large and small.

Will God be enough for me if my child doesn't get well?

Will God be enough for me if a job doesn't come through for me the way I hope?

Will God be enough for me if my spouse doesn't come home? If my life is suddenly axed in half?

If I look at the terrain of my life and let myself return to the most painful places, and realize that God was there, looking on, choosing not to block my path, not to barricade me from excruciating assaults, can I believe He is still strong and good and kind?

For many of us, far too often, the answer to that question is this: "I don't know."

We don't really know if God is going to be enough for us.

Because we don't really know God.

His voice is not familiar to us. If we've heard it at all, it was so soft we could hardly distinguish it from our culture's pounding cacophony. Our fears have drowned it. Our pride has mocked it. Our inattention has shoved it into a boring monotone, unidentifiable from the other voices that drone in the background of everyday living.

His arms may have felt like vices, holding us away from fun and pleasure.

His music seemed like a dirge, not a two-step.

Because we don't know Him as He really is.

We haven't learned what He's really like.

We haven't discovered His beauty and majesty. We haven't really let ourselves be drawn into the mystery and adventure that is the gospel.

Exposing the Impostor

In C. S. Lewis's final book in the Narnia Chronicles, *The Last Battle,* he tells the story of an ape who invents a huge deception.

Using a lion hide discarded by a hunter, the ape drapes it over a donkey and parades him through Narnia, pretending the donkey is the great king Aslan. Of course, anyone getting too close to the donkey would see that he's a fake, so the ape hides him in a stall and brings him out only at night to let the citizens view his silhouette against the light of a bonfire.

During the day, the ape sits outside the stall, dressed in ridiculous finery, and pretends to speak for Aslan, making cruel, self-serving demands of the Narnians and imposing a harsh rule. The citizens' lives become unbearable. They grow bitter against Aslan, blaming him for their bondage and misery.

The deception is successful for a while, but suddenly, the plot pivots. Because there are those who know the real Aslan. They know his heart. They know the story of the White Witch and the long years of winter with no Christmases. They know the story of the stone slab where the lion died, and how he took up his life again and went to battle to kill the witch and bring spring to Narnia.

Those who know Aslan know he is not to blame for the evil that is abroad in Narnia. Instead of being angry at *him*, they direct their anger at the imposter, at the evil ape who is pretending to be the king. They join with others who know the real king, and they fight to bring the truth to those in bondage.

Because they know Aslan is the only one who can make sense of their misery. He's the only one who can relieve it.

It's a great tale of swords and knives and castles and towers and young kings and children and talking animals. It is a wild story of slaves and warriors and grand escapades. It is the gospel retold—the gospel of Jesus Christ, our Aslan, who took on the imposter in our world, the "prince of the power of the air." This was the imposter who entered the garden and convinced Adam and Eve that God was a liar. This imposter robbed us of Eden and set himself up as the king and took earth's inhabitants into bondage.

The gospel is the story of how Jesus fought and died for our freedom. It's the story of how Satan was exposed for the fraud that he is when Jesus walked away from the empty tomb.

Those who know the story, who know Jesus, who know His heart, know that He is not to blame for the misery that still is present in our world. He is the only one who can make sense of it. He is the only one who can relieve it. The one and only omnipotent King, He alone can direct the events of the universe and make the outcome a glorious one. He alone is sovereign, the Creator-King, the One to whom all authority is given in heaven and on the earth.

We, His creatures, are hurled into a grand narrative. Like hobbits caught up in an adventure not of our own making, we tumble into dangers and ferocious encounters, characters in a plot we didn't write for ourselves. We are not the authors, we are not the screenwriters. Yet God has written us into the script, making our stories essential to the telling of *His* story, the story of God.

Through the telling, God's reveals His heart. His goodness and mercy sing on the page as He shows His pity for a people in bondage to a liar. His ferocity explodes as He battles the imposter; His love and compassion captivate our imagination as we see Him come to us, speak with us, rescue us, and plan a future for us so perfect, so full of joy and majesty that we cannot wrap our minds around the glory of it. And to accomplish it all, He must be able to command the universe to do His bidding.

> But this is knowledge which Christians today largely lack: and that is one reason why our faith is so feeble and our worship so flabby. We are modern men, and modern men, though they cherish great thoughts of man, have as a rule small thoughts of God.[3]

When pain seeps into our hearts, when horror haunts our footsteps, when it seems as though Narnia's king has been usurped by an ape, our comfort will be found in the truth of God's sovereignty. We will find our hope and joy in large thoughts—not *small*—about our God.

As a Child

Daniel wrote that "the Most High is sovereign over the kingdoms of men" (Daniel 4:25).

Whatever rule we may think we exert, God overrules.

Whatever heights we may think we have achieved, God is higher still, beyond measuring.

"The earth is the LORD's, and everything in it, the world and all who live in it" (Psalm 24:1).

"Heaven is my throne, and the earth is my footstool," God declares (Isaiah 66:1).

Ours is not a small God.

Maybe we would have a better idea of how large He is if we did not think ourselves so large.

The heroes and heroines of Lewis's Narnia tales are children not yet out of grammar school—and not just because it makes for better telling. Children have always been at the center of the gospel.

"Become like a child if you want to know Me and experience My kingdom," Jesus told the disciples (see Luke 18:16).

Become childlike in your thinking. Live with the kind of simple expectancy that children have—the kind of wide-eyed wonder that sends them clambering into a wardrobe, dashing into adventures that older, more sophisticated thinkers refuse to enter.

The children stumble into dangers and delightful escapades, all the while enchanted by nothing less than a huge lion, the king Aslan, whom they both love and fear, who both charms and terrifies them. They are shy, yet at the same time irresistibly drawn by his power and majesty.

Maybe it's because they haven't yet grown large enough to think of themselves as kings.

David wrote in Psalms: "You are awesome, O God!" (68:35).

"I have made the Sovereign LORD my refuge; I will tell of all your deeds" (73:28).

"Praise be to the LORD God, the God of Israel, who alone does marvelous deeds. Praise be to his glorious name forever; may the whole earth be filled with his glory" (72:18).

Looking up at the heavens, David felt his smallness. "What is man that you are mindful of him, the son of man that you care for him?" (8:4).

David saw himself as a tiny speck of dust on this planet formed by the God he worshiped. He saw his frailty; he bowed before the sovereignty of his Creator and lived adventures that we still talk about today.

"[I am] like a weaned child," David sang (131:2). Not a mighty man who can dictate to the sovereign God—but a child, resting in the arms of one greater, one stronger than he. One on whom he was dependent.

Here's what we have to understand: We can't fully enter into the comfort of God's sovereignty unless we become as little children, unless we recognize His full authority and accept it with childlike trust.

But it's a challenge for us, isn't it? We don't like the idea of being dependent. We spend our whole lives seeking *independence*. Our American way of life is committed to ensuring our right to autonomy. We've fought wars to protect our right to govern ourselves. We fight every day to ensure that we are free to make our own decisions. Because we are a people committed to the vote.

But in God's family, kids don't get to vote.

By virtue of His sovereignty, God makes the decisions about our lives, about His universe. His decrees aren't ours to debate. We can forget about appealing His rulings to a higher court—there *is* no higher court.

The only decision that's ours is this: to quarrel, or not to quarrel.

Quarreling with Sovereignty

Isaiah gave us a picture of how silly it is to argue with God: "Woe to him who quarrels with his Maker, to him who is but a potsherd among the potsherds on the ground. Does the clay say to the potter, 'What are you making?'" (Isaiah 45:9).

Imagine a chunk of clay grappling with the artisan whose hands are pinching and pressing it. Close your eyes and visualize this: The clod of mud, lying in the Potter's hands, struggling to find limbs to wrestle with the Potter, demanding to be shaped in a certain way. Absurd, isn't it?

The imagery gets even better. Imagine the clay demanding to be heard in a court of law, insisting on a ruling that would give it authority over the Potter. Can the creature find evidence enough to convince a judge that the creature, not the Creator, is qualified and competent to run the universe?

I love this passage from a Puritan preacher's sermon:

> When chaff strives against the wind, stubble
> against the fire . . . when clay strives against the
> potter, when man strives against God, it is easy to
> know on which side the victory will go.[4]

We can quarrel with God (which we all do at times), but keep this in mind: God always wins. "The earth is the LORD's, and everything in it, the world, and all who live in it" (Psalm 24:1).

It's all His to do with as He pleases. There is no quark uncharted and no star unnamed. There is no black hole He has not measured; no ocean depth He hasn't probed. There is no one higher to consult about the planets and the stars—if they should burn out or explode and expand. There's not another authority to advise God on whether Mount St. Helen's should erupt again, or whether the earth should quake and crack open.

The Lord is "the Most High God" (Daniel 4:2). There just isn't anyone any higher on the ladder to consult. The buck stops at the throne of God.

Dallas Willard wrote, "If God is running the universe and has first claim on our lives, guess who *isn't* running the universe and does not get to have things as they please."[5]

And that's the rub, of course. God gets to choose; we don't.

A View from the Pasture

We are the sheep of His pasture (Psalm 100:3).

His pasture. Not ours.

He's the shepherd; we're not.

We're woolly, smelly, silly, defenseless, and dependent creatures. The pastures we wander in are not ours. He brings us onto His terrain, releases us to run and chase and explore. But always, He remains in charge. Because He owns it—all of it.

But He is good. And that's what we cannot forget, even for a moment.

"I am the good shepherd," Jesus said (John 10:11).

He was telling His disciples, "I am not a hireling. This isn't just a part-time job for Me; it's My life's calling."

"I'm the real thing," He was saying. "And here's how you'll know: When danger strikes, I'll be the one who saves you. If it ever comes down to My life or yours, I'll be the one who dies, not you."

Don't be confused by an imposter, Jesus was saying. Oh, one will show up from time to time, lurking near the sheep pen, or ducking behind a boulder in the pasture somewhere, just waiting to steal the flock from the shepherd.

He might be able to pretend to care. He might even find you a spot of yellowed grass once in a while, and make you feel like you've had something to eat. He might take you to a puddle for a drink, but your thirst will not be quenched. And when life gets scary and dangerous for you, when you're on a precipice and you feel yourself sliding toward the edge, it is only the Good Shepherd who will reach out to grab you and hold you against His heart and whisper words of love and comfort.

Only the true Shepherd will give His life in exchange for yours. The imposter will give you up to save himself.

There is only One you can trust with your life here and now, only One you can trust with eternity—because there is only One who is sovereign.

J. I. Packer wrote:

> The vision of God's sovereignty is enormously
> strengthening. To know that nothing happens in
> God's world apart from God's will may frighten the
> godless, but it stabilizes the saints, assuring them
> that God has everything worked out and that
> everything that happens has meaning,
> whether or not we can see it at the time. . . .

> Knowing that God is on the throne upholds us under
> pressure and in the face of bewilderment, pain,
> hostility, and events that seem to make no sense.[6]

The truth of God's sovereignty will stabilize those who are childlike in their trust; those who know they are too small to take care of themselves; those who know that He is large enough to take care of everything.

It will stabilize those who know the Shepherd is good. It will stabilize those who know His heart.

A Part in the Story

God doesn't forget about us.

He doesn't disregard us.

The Sovereign of the universe who is steadily sending forth the marching orders for history's unfolding doesn't rule with only the occasional thought of us coming to mind.

> In His vast indomitable rule, He considers what is
> good for us, what is best. Whether we like it or not,
> God intends to give us what we need, not what
> we now think we want. Once more, we are
> embarrassed by the intolerable compliment,
> by too much love, not too little.[7]
>
> —C. S. LEWIS

Imagine! The King of Kings whose word keeps the constellations in place, whose authority orders the waves to the shore, and no further; whose sovereignty shifts the tectonic plates of the earth and drives the rivers into lakes; whose rule brings down rain and sweeps up cities with the wind—this great King counts the hairs on our heads and takes into account our breaths, our heartbeats. He considers our sufferings and sorrows. He paints them into the portrait of His sovereign grace, making them a cause for glory, not shame.

Listen again to C. S. Lewis:

> Over a sketch made idly to amuse a child, an artist
> may not take much trouble; he may be content to let it
> go even though it is not exactly as he meant it to be.
> But over the great picture of his life—the work which
> he loves, though in a different fashion, as intensely as
> a man loves a woman or a mother a child—
> he will take endless trouble.[8]

The creator of time and space, of all things material and immaterial, God reveals Himself to us in terms familiar to us, as artist and storyteller.

As He moves across the pages of history past and yet to come, God takes "endless trouble" with us. He remembers that we are small. He doesn't rewrite the story to accommodate our size. Instead, He brings us into the hugeness of the eternal tale and gives us a voice in the telling.

Oh, "intolerable compliment!" that God would let us find our names written, our stories mingled with His in the grand story of redemption!

Those who know Him, who know His story, know that "the LORD our God is righteous in everything he does" (Daniel 9:14).

When the world looks scary and dangerous and everything in our lives seems to be tottering on the edge of cataclysm, those who know God don't blame Him for the ugliness and sorrow in the world. They know the difference between the Lion of Judah and the puppet regime of an ape and a donkey wearing a lion's hide. They know that Aslan is on the move, and that their suffering will be relieved one day. They know that in the meantime, they can trust His sovereign rule and travel in His train with confidence, knowing His heart is good.

In a scene from *The Last Battle,* when the children face a moment of great fear, one wiser than they are reminds them, "But courage, child: we are all between the paws of the true Aslan."[9]

That's where we are, all of us. At times, we'll feel terror; at times peace. But always we are in the place of greatest safety, the place that is the best of all places to be.

> Yet we do trust our God; we do believe that if there had been anything better than what is, that better thing would have been chosen for us. We do believe that when we look back at the end of the journey we shall see how perfect the way was—every mile of it.[10]
>
> —AMY CARMICHAEL

Welcoming Sovereignty

Mary dared to look back, dared to consider her pain in the context of God's sovereign rule. And then, in childlike faith, she entrusted herself to the Father's love. She trusted herself to the goodness of His heart.

It is goodness that recognizes that our finite minds can't always see what is best, can seldom make out what is *good* versus what is good *for us,* and for the kingdom of God, and for His glory.

It is sovereign goodness that steps in to guarantee that *actual* good is accomplished, not the inferior brand of what "feels good" that our fickle hearts would choose, if left to themselves.

Eugene Peterson wrote, "The basic conviction of a

Christian is that God intends good for us and that He will get His way in us."[11]

God will get His way, because He is the Most High God, and it is His pleasure to rule and reign in power, wisdom, and love.

When confusion wreaks havoc in our minds, when pain pulses and fear taunts, we have only two choices: We can trust ourselves to the sovereign rule of the Most High God, or fight and wrangle with Him until we grow bitter and hardhearted. One or the other will be the outcome. These are our only options.

We can choose to trust in childlike faith, knowing that "as often as we make that choice, everything, even the most trivial things, become new. Our little lives become great—part of the mysterious work of God's salvation. Once that happens, nothing is accident, casual, or futile anymore. Even the most insignificant event speaks the language of faith, hope, and above all else, love."[12]

We can choose to believe that "God is in ultimate control of the world, from the largest international intrigue to the smallest bird-fall in the forest."[13]

We can believe, with David:

Though I walk in the midst of trouble, you preserve my life;
You stretch out your hand against the anger of my foes,
with your right hand you save me.
The LORD will fulfill his purpose for me;
Your love, O LORD, endures forever—
do not abandon the works of your hands.
—PSALM 138:7–8

We can believe, with the apostle Paul, that God has "placed all things under his feet and appointed him to be head over evrything" (Ephesians 1:22). Even now, at this very moment, "in all things God works for the good of those who love him, who have been called according to his purpose" (Romans 8:28).

We can believe that God is mindful of us; that He takes into account our smallness; that He takes "endless trouble" over us; that He does not disregard us from His lofty throne; and that He will be faithful to His promise to make all things new (see Revelation 21).

We can believe God, or we can quarrel with Him.

We can embrace His sovereignty and feel His arms come around us.

We can wrestle with God's rule, or welcome it—this is the choice we face when catastrophe strikes us. If we know God, if we know His heart, the choice will come easy.

And who would want to skip town when God is inviting us to stay and dance?

TRACKING GRACE

> TO SAY THAT GOD IS SOVEREIGN IS TO DECLARE THAT
> HE IS THE ALMIGHTY, THE POSSESSOR OF ALL POWER IN
> HEAVEN AND EARTH, SO THAT NO ONE CAN DEFEAT HIS
> COUNSELS, THWART HIS PURPOSE, OR RESIST HIS WILL.[14]
> —ARTHUR PINK

> *But he stands alone, and who can oppose him?*
> *He does whatever he pleases.*
> —JOB 23:13

1. How might you need to adjust your idea of God's character in order to be comforted by His sovereignty?

2. What circumstances in your life have challenged you to examine God's sovereignty?

3. What does it mean to you to think that God, with all His power and authority, is "mindful" of you?

4. In what way do you see the need for childlikeness in response to God's sovereignty?

5. What would your life be like if you resolved to live according to the belief that God is sovereign?

CHURCHES ARE NOT ONLY AWE
INSPIRING; THEY ARE ODD
INSPIRING, ATTRACTING AN
EARTHY ASSORTMENT OF JESUS'
FOLLOWERS. THE STAINED
GLASS IS EXTRAORDINARY, BUT
IT IS ALSO COVERED WITH OR-
DINARY FINGERPRINTS.[1]

MICHAEL YACONELLI

Accept one another, then, just as Christ accepted
you, in order to bring praise to God.

—ROMANS 15:7

CHAPTER NINE

Body Heat

LIVING IN THE
FELLOWSHIP OF BELIEVERS

I was making the slow, steep climb up a cobbled street in old Quebec City when a young man approached me with a tin can, speaking soft and rapid French. I shook my head and smiled. "No Francais."

"Inglais?"

I nodded.

He dove into a hodgepodge of English-French, saying he was collecting donations for troubled kids. He could have been their poster boy.

He wore a long ponytail, several tattoos, and white and red fingernail polish. His clothing made a loud grunge-punk fashion statement, and except for the fish symbol dangling from a leather cord around his neck, I might have walked past him.

"Are you a Christian?" I asked.

"Christian? You mean born again, yes? I'm a Christian! Yes, yes! Are you born again?"

For the next half hour, tourists and locals rushed by us, sometimes pushing us out of the way as a middle-aged Texas tourist and French-Canadian rebel-punk chatted on a crowded street corner.

"I was a drug addict," he said, gesturing toward the veins in his arms. He mimed shooting heroin.

"I lost everything—my girlfriend, my daughter. One night I heard about Jesus when a preacher came to the park across the street. I walked through the crowd to pray with him. Jesus came into my heart!"

He pressed his hand to his chest and beamed.

"I tell people about Jesus all the time." He gestured to the crowds on the narrow street. "Sometimes they think I'm crazy, but I know He's here." He patted his chest again. "But it's hard for me. I feel, how you say it? Tempted?"

I grinned. "Yeah, I know what that feels like."

His friends aren't Christians, he told me. Their dangerous lifestyle includes all the things we can imagine, and, I'd guess, some we can't begin to imagine.

"I don't do that anymore. I'm tempted sometimes—my skin, you know, it's weak." He pinched his tattooed forearms.

"Your skin? Oh, okay, your flesh."

"*Oui*, my flesh—it's weak."

"Do you have a Bible?" I asked.

"Oh, yes, I love the Bible," he said. "You know Acts?"

Groping for the right English words, he grew excited as he told me, "I have the Holy Spirit! I know Jesus loves me, but I have trouble." He shook his head and grimaced. "It's hard to find work. My friends want me to go to Montreal next month to make—how you say it?—a porno movie, triple-x. I could make a lot of money. My spirit says no, but my skin—" again, he pinched his forearm, "it is weak."

Suddenly, the conversation turned urgent.

"What's your name?" I asked.

"Louis.*"

I could feel love for this young man spilling into my heart, so much love my chest ached with the weight of it.

"You know you can't make that film, don't you, Louis? No matter how much money you might get paid, it's not worth the cost to your soul."

With a Gallic shrug, he smiled sadly.

"Do you really believe God loves you, Louis?"

"Yes, yes."

"Do you think He can take care of you?"

He nodded, his ponytail bobbing, his eyes wide. "Once, I had no money, no place to live. God helped me. I know He can take care of me."

"Do you understand *fellowship*?" I asked him.

He frowned.

"Do you have a church or a group of Christian friends to encourage you?" I asked.

Louis became animated, like an actor who stumbled onto a stage and found a willing audience. "No church. I tried. They ask me questions—where do you come from, what do you do, are you a drug addict? I tell them the truth, they move away. They don't like how I look." He pointed to his ink-stained skin. "They don't want me there. I think I scare them."

I could imagine the stir he might create in a congregation unused to seeing messy, tattooed, long-haired young men with red and white nail polish seated in their pews.

---

*not his real name

I know there are such churches—I've been a part of them.

I've been the one who wanted to move to another pew, upwind, not down. I've wanted to close the door on the Sunday school classroom so that the unkempt latecomer meandering down the hall would choose the class next door, instead of the one I'm in.

Because dealing with the unclean and unsightly, the messy, is unsettling, scary, and off-putting.

Because I didn't understand what the church is all about.

I didn't understand that, of all the places on the face of the earth, the church is the one place where someone like Louis should find welcome.

It is, after all, the place that welcomed someone like me.

None Righteous

"We *all* like sheep, have gone astray," wrote Isaiah (53:6, italics added).

In Romans, Paul wrote to those "loved by God and called to be saints," reminding us *all* that "there is no one righteous, not even one" (1:7, 3:10). Are we any better? Not at all! In his second letter to the Corinthians he reminds believers that, because of Christ's death, "We don't evaluate people by what they have or how they look" (5:16 THE MESSAGE).

And against that reality, the New Testament teaches us to get together, and don't ever stop, because we need each other (Hebrews 10:25).

We need each other in those times when old friends try to pull us back into the lifestyle we had before we knew Christ.

We need each other when temptation is so strong that, left to ourselves, we'll succumb.

We need each other when life is overwhelming and crises are bearing down on us with pressure so great we feel like we're going to be crushed.

Not one of us, from the eldest Christian to the most recent convert still agog with the joy of new birth, can stand alone, or serve alone, or enjoy the sweetness of the life of Christ in isolation.

God never intended for any of us to travel alone. Somehow we forget that. Or we ignore it.

And people like Louis get left behind. Sometimes we get left behind. Sometimes we're the ones doing the leaving, because we don't understand what the church is all about.

Christ's Vision

Imagine a place you can walk into and be greeted with genuine love and welcomed with open arms. Imagine, there among people who know you, but *still* love you, you feel free to say you're in real trouble at work, or at home, and no one says, "What's wrong with you?"

No one says, "I can't sit here with someone like you."

No one says, "Too bad, buddy, but we've got better things to do than listen to your problems."

Imagine a place where you can take your confusion and doubts and dump them in a pile in the middle of the room and not be made to feel ashamed. Where others just like you feel free to say, "Yeah, I've doubted too. In fact, I'm not sure about anything right now. I could use some encouragement too."

Is there a place where people are willing to acknowledge their own weaknesses and are humble enough, courageous enough, to say, "Let's pray about your marriage (or your job, or your kids) right here, right now"?

Imagine people talking together about what God desires for their lives; people committed to encouraging each other to listen to God and obey and trust Him.

Imagine being in community with people who will surround you with prayer and kindness, speaking hope and peace, when death or illness strikes your family.

Imagine being in community with people who gently, but boldly, come to you and warn you about behaviors that threaten your family and your soul. Imagine them knowing you well enough and caring enough to say, "This is wrong! Don't go that way!"

Imagine knowing they are guided by deep love for Christ, and for you, and wisdom from His Word and His Holy Spirit. Imagine knowing that they don't want to hurt you, but they take to heart God's instructions to "teach and admonish one another with all wisdom" (Colossians 3:15–17).

Imagine being a part of a community like that.

This is what Christ envisioned the church to be. Just like that: a community of believers who take seriously what God says; a community committed to living out the reality of the invisible truths of God together.

Is there such a place?

Shared Lives

For years, I wondered.

I believed the doctrine of the church—that there exists a mysterious relationship between Christ and all believers, a relationship that needs the metaphor of marriage to explain it (Ephesians 5:32).

I believed in the church universal, one body that represents the Bride of Christ, for whom He died and rose again, for whom He will one day return and take to His home in heaven for eternal joy and fellowship.

I believed the theology, but I didn't fully enter into the reality of it until I joined the Grace class.

I wrote the story of the Grace class in a chapter about the discipline of fellowship in an earlier book, *Intimate Faith*.[2] The story continues to unfold. Week after week, I enter the classroom on the second floor of the Christian Learning Center at my church, and I find myself in the company of people who listen to me, and sometimes warn me. A couple of them get in my face at times, teaching me, encouraging me, but always loving me, imperfectly, but intentionally, and with desire for my good. Sometimes I am able to warn them, or encourage them, or simply love them when what they need more than anything is hugging.

I'm learning what it means to be members of one body, fellow heirs with Christ, family.

I'm learning that, while there is a church universal that includes all races, all nations, the only way to live in the reality of that church is to be a part of a small group.

John Eldredge wrote:

> Certainly, the body of Christ is a vast throng, millions of people around the globe. But when Scripture talks about church, it means community. The little fellowships of the heart that are outposts of the kingdom. A shared life. They worship together, eat together, pray for one another, go on quests together. They hang out together in each other's homes. . . . And *every* chronicle of war or quest will tell you that the men and women who fought so bravely fought *for each other*. That's where the acts of heroism and sacrifice take place because that's where the devotion is.

You simply cannot be devoted to a mass of people;
devotion takes place in small units, just as in a family.
. . . Whatever else you do, you *must* have a small
fellowship to walk with you and fight with you
and bandage your wounds.[3]

Is it simply a practical matter of safety and cama-
raderie?

Or is it something more?

A Messy Tradition

Think of what you'd say to your family if you knew it
was the last hour you would spend with them.

I know what I'd say. I'd say take care of each other.
Stay close, and be there for one another.

I'd say help each other remember what's eternal,
what's of greatest value; remember what our family has
been about. Love one another.

That's what I'd say.

Nothing else would matter to me. I wouldn't care if
they got rich, or famous, or if they grew powerful. The
only thing that matters to me is that they stay a family; that
they continue to walk in faith, that they look after one another and love one another, because that's what families do.

Now look at what was in Jesus' heart in the hours before His crucifixion. In His prayer in John 17, you hear
His heartbeat for His disciples, whom He called His
friends and His family (Mark 3:34–35). He yearns for their
unity, their oneness—that they will take care of each other; that they will be united in living out the purposes of the
kingdom of God; that they will live in the fullness of the
love of God; that they will see themselves, and each other,
as the gift God the Father gave the Son.

Be a family, He was telling them. Look after one another. Remember what I've been about, agree on the essentials. Work together. Love one another.

Because this describes the relationship enjoyed by the Trinity—the Father, the Son, and the Holy Spirit.

"Let us make man in *our* image," God said (Genesis 1:26, italics added). It is an image that is incomplete without fellowship, without unity.

Jesus said, "I pray also for those who will believe in me through their message, that all of them may be one, Father, just as you are in me and I am in you" (John 17:20–21).

This is what life looks like within the Trinity—immeasurable love, unity of purpose, fellowship, and oneness that is so mysterious it cannot be fully explained in any human language.

And it is a mystery we are called into.

It is the mystery of the church.

How did the mystery become a horror story for so many?

How is it that this divine organism is so often viewed, and so often behaves, like an elite organization that only the clean and well dressed can join? An organization that is offended by the likes of a Louis, and others like him?

Maybe it's because, when we're all dressed up to play church, we are able to camouflage the truth about ourselves; we can pretend that we're not all misfits just like Louis. But strip us of our respectable clothes and good manners and our Christian vocabulary with its clichés, and we can't pretend any longer. It's obvious to everyone that we aren't any better, "not at all," than any other person who stands in need of the imputed righteousness of Jesus Christ. We're all a mess.

Michael Yaconelli wrote:

> You might say Christianity has a tradition of messy
> spirituality. Messy prophets, messy kings, messy dis-
> ciples, messy apostles. From God's people getting
> into one mess after another in the Old Testament to
> most of the New Testament's being written to
> straighten out messes in the church, the Bible pre-
> sents a glorious story of a very messy faith.[4]

How is it that Christians can read the Bible so often
and miss this? Where do we get the idea that the church is
a place for people who've got it all together, for people
whose lives aren't messy?

I wish I could have brought Louis home with me to the
Grace class. Oh, his appearance would have raised a few
eyebrows and garnered a few curious frowns, but overall,
he would have been welcomed by men and women who are
open and honest, vulnerable about their lives and their
struggles. He would find himself loved among those of us
who are facing marriage crises, addictions that aren't
easily cured, bankruptcy, terminal illness, troubled children, sick and aging parents, and mental illness. We are
singles, couples, widows, divorcees, some young, some
older. We are a motley crew, but we've figured this out:
We can't make it alone. And so we gather each week, and
often in between, to offer each other support and love and
encouragement.

We're not perfect, nor is the larger church we're a part
of—as a body, we've had our problems, what church
hasn't? Some are ongoing. But somehow, this message is
penetrating our congregation and finding expression in
our small groups: We are a people entrusted with the mission to live out the reality of Jesus Christ, the Savior who

ate supper with reprobates, who spoke kindly to prostitutes; the Savior who touched lepers and beggars with the same hands that greeted noblemen and cooked a shore breakfast for His closest friends.

We are a people who are learning the value of community —sometimes falteringly, always imperfectly. Feelings get hurt; anger erupts. But forgiveness happens too, and gestures of reconciliation.

Like the time a class member was hurt when the larger group scheduled an event that, because of her work schedule, left her out. She felt disregarded, devalued. It was a sensitive time, a time of withdrawal, silence, anger and frustration. But reconciliation occurred. It happened like this: The parties involved talked and talked and prayed and prayed; and the rest of us prayed too. And then one Sunday we walked into class and there on the podium was a large package, gift wrapped from the injured party to the director of the class—the guy she had been so angry with.

"We've made peace," the gift said, without anyone saying a word.

The image of that package sticks with me. I see it when I read Jesus' prayer to His Father, when He calls us "those whom you gave me out of the world. They were yours; you gave them to me" (John 17:6).

We are the Father's gift to the Son—each of us, *all* of us.

Sometimes the gift wrapping is a little tattered, a bit messy—little more than a brown bag and twine—but Jesus considered the contents inside a priceless treasure worth dying for.

And He expects us to value it as well and treat it with tender care.

Human Hands

Leslie is too young to have a stroke. Strokes happen to grandparents, great-aunts and great-uncles, not to young, healthy women just in off the ski slopes. But, it seems, catastrophe is an indiscriminate caller. And it struck shortly after Christmas as Leslie and her family were driving home to Dallas from Colorado, as she was reading a story to her children to help pass the time and the miles.

What happened next is a series of miracles: how the nearest hospital was equipped to care for her; how her husband made contact with a doctor-friend in Dallas who knew the doctor in Pueblo and reassured the young family that they were in good, capable hands; how God allowed Leslie to recover completely from the stroke.

As I listened to the account of Leslie's ordeal, I was awed by the perfection of God's care for His child. In every detail of the crisis, God's hand was obvious, from the instant one side of her body went numb and limp to the moment they saw the sign and the exit ramp for the nearest hospital—a hospital with a sign saying "Stroke Unit." Entering the emergency room, Leslie was the only patient; her care was quick and efficient—the doctor on duty was the head of neurology.

Leslie's life will be forever marked by the stroke, but not disabled by it.

Catastrophes do that: They mark our lives.

And so does God's care.

And never more so than when that care is administered by the loving hands of God's people.

Henri Nouwen wrote:

> No one person can fulfill all your needs. But the community can truly hold you. The community can

let you experience the fact that, beyond
your anguish, there are human hands that
hold you and show you God's love.[5]

The human community showed Leslie God's love, starting with the moment her church in Dallas got the phone call telling them what had happened. A contact was made with a church in Pueblo, and Christians there started praying.

In Dallas, Christians went to work to help with practical matters. Leslie's parents had been in Colorado with the family, and they brought the children home to Dallas while Leslie remained hospitalized in Pueblo. Friends in Dallas helped with child care, the car pool, after school activities, and all the busyness that goes with having three active school-age children.

When Leslie was finally released, she came home to find that all her Christmas decorations had been boxed up and stored away in shiny new red and green boxes; the house was stocked with food and bursting with flower arrangements. Anything that could be done to ease Leslie and her family during a difficult, frightening time had been done. And it seemed someone was always looking for something more to do.

I read Leslie's thank-you letter to the community that so tenderly, lovingly cared for her and her family. She wrote, "Thank you for growing up a body of believers that knows how to minister to those in need."

Leslie understands this: It takes a "growing up."

That's what Paul understood when he wrote to the Colossian church, "I am struggling for you" (2:1). He agonized over them in prayer, ached for them to fully understand the mystery of the church and be united in love, encouraged and full of complete understanding, living in the wisdom and knowledge of Jesus Christ.

Read through Paul's letters to all the New Testament churches and hear the same theme: Grow up!

Live like adults, not children. Stop quarreling. Be gentle. Don't be prejudiced. Be wise in the way you treat outsiders. Don't miss opportunities to show God's love and share His gospel.

Avoid silly controversies.

Know truth.

Live pure lives. Forgive as Christ forgave you.

Live peacefully with one another.

And "over all these virtues, put on love, which binds them all together in perfect unity" (Colossians 3:14).

There it is again—the theme of unity: Oneness of heart, directed and powered by love. Oneness expressed in community.

Impossible Dream

We were playing an "icebreaker" game at a women's retreat. Everybody had to write down one dream they'd like to see fulfilled before they die. Then we had to try to match the dream with the person who wrote it.

Who dreamed of visiting Tuscany before she died?

Who dreamed of finishing her college degree?

Who dreamed of owning a lake house like the one we were using for the retreat?

Who dreamed of a Christmas dinner where all her adult children arrived on time, in a good mood, ready to enjoy the day without picking at each other and ruining the festivities? No sarcasm, no cruel reminders of past mistakes and past misbehavior. No impatience. No rivalries. Just a nice, pleasant family meal with all tensions checked at the door.

Talk about an impossible dream! We all agreed everyone of us would probably get to Tuscany by rowboat before any of us would enjoy a holiday dinner without some level of tension.

But we all agreed we dream of it.

We yearn for it.

Now, remember what was in Jesus' heart. Then read the account of the Last Supper: disciples vying for the place of power—"I get to sit next to Jesus in the kingdom!"

"No, I do!"

"I'm the best disciple!"

"No, I am!"

Peek into the room and see Jesus celebrating the Passover with His disciples, His last "family dinner," and see a traitor plotting, brothers quarreling, Peter boasting, and all twelve of them misunderstanding Jesus' message and His mission.

Life in community wasn't easy then. It isn't easy now. But God's desire for it hasn't lessened.

He yearns to see the beauty and unity of His triune nature lived out here and now among us, His body. He yearns for us to love one another as the Son and the Father and Spirit love and adore one another.

He yearns for us be together, of one mind and one spirit, in expressing the truth of His gospel and the reality of His character.

Dietrich Bonhoeffer wrote, "The more genuine and the deeper our community becomes, the more will everything else between us recede, the more clearly and purely will Jesus Christ and His work become the one and only thing that is vital between us."[6]

We are a family, yes, but we are also a community living under the imperative of a "divine call." We are a community Henri Nouwen described as a "waiting community." We live together with "common expectation"; we reject the idea of a "cozy clique" or a "safe shelter."[7] We live instead with a kind of holy expectation, always looking forward to what is to come—a grand family dinner when no one will be late and no one will be preoccupied with selfish pursuits or cravings for personal greatness. We all will be caught up in the beauty and perfection of Jesus, our host. Enjoying Him will be our only interest. Loving Him will consume us.

Until then, Nouwen continued, God calls us to understand and live in the truth that "by our common call to the New Jerusalem we recognize each other on the road as brothers and sisters."[8]

Even if the brother is covered with tattoos and sporting red and white nail polish.

Even if he used to be a drug addict.

A Gift of Grace

Bonhoeffer heard the prison doors clang behind him in 1943 and knew that the life of fellowship he enjoyed and cherished as a part of a community of believers would never be the same. A rebel-preacher who dared to defy the Third Reich, he spent two years in German prisons, charged with plotting to assassinate Hitler. On April 9, 1945, he was hanged as a traitor.

His words live on:

> How inexhaustible are the riches that open up for
> those who by God's will are privileged to live in the
> daily fellowship of life with other Christians!
> It is true, of course, that what is an unspeakable gift
> of God for the lonely individual is easily disregarded
> and trodden under foot by those who have the gift
> every day. It is easily forgotten that the fellowship of

Christian brethren is a gift of grace. . . . It is grace,
nothing but grace that we are allowed to live in community with Christian brethren.[9]

I think of Louis often. Before we said *au revoir,* we talked about grace—the meaning is the same in French as it is in English.

"You learn a lot about grace when you make yourself a part of a group of Christians," I said. "It's like God's arms come around you when His people hug you. His love becomes more real to you when His people share their lives with you."

Louis understood.

"But I think you could teach a church something about grace too, Louis," I added. "You know, the church needs you as much as you need the church."

He smiled and looked at me intently. "Can I see your eyes?" he asked, and he reached toward my face and slid my sunglasses down my nose.

Tears choked me.

He touched my shoulders lightly and leaned forward to kiss me on both cheeks in the purest, sweetest of European gestures. I couldn't speak.

Locals and sightseers bumped against us. Noisy tour buses belched past us. But the bustle of old Quebec City faded as I stood there, thinking, *This is what it's all about, isn't it, Lord? Being the body of Christ, loving one another, fighting for one another, serving and caring for one another because we are brothers and sisters, children of the Father— it's about being Your family.*

"I'll pray for you," I promised Louis. "Don't forget you're a child of the King, and you really do have lots of brothers and sisters out there. You don't have to go it alone."

I walked away, comforted by his promise to look up a local pastor who once had been kind to him. I recalled a time in my own life when *I* had been determined to go it alone. But through time and experience, and the powerful work of the Holy Spirit, I grew to love the body of Christ and to understand my desperate need for it. I learned that living apart from a local fellowship of believers is like living alone in a cold place. It is like huddling on an ice flow, shivering in misery, when you could leap onto a solid shore and warm yourself with others who have learned there is a deeper meaning to the phrase "body heat."

✒ TRACKING GRACE

THE PHYSICAL PRESENCE OF OTHER CHRISTIANS IS A SOURCE OF INCOMPARABLE JOY AND STRENGTH TO THE BELIEVER. . . . THE CHRISTIAN NEEDS ANOTHER CHRISTIAN WHO SPEAKS GOD'S WORD TO HIM. HE NEEDS HIM AGAIN AND AGAIN WHEN HE BECOMES UNCERTAIN AND DISCOURAGED.[10]

—DIETRICH BONHOEFFER

How good and pleasant it is when brothers live
together in unity!

—PSALM 133:1

1. Does your experience with a local body of be-
    lievers differ from what you see as Jesus' intent?
    If so, how?

2. Knowing what Jesus desires for us to experience
    in fellowship, what changes might be needed in
    your heart in order for that to happen?

3. How would your local fellowship respond if
    Louis showed up for worship Sunday morning?
    How would you respond?

4. What does it mean to you to think in terms of
    "messy spirituality"? Are you comforted or
    offended?

PRAYER IS SUFFERING'S

BEST RESULT.[1]

EUGENE PETERSON

The LORD has heard my cry for mercy;
the LORD accepts my prayer.

—PSALM 6:9

Chapter Ten

The Great Art

CONVERSATION WITH GOD

When life is a mess, the first thing I do is pray.

Isn't that what most of us do?

Jesus said we should pray. The apostles tell us to pray. The Old Testament is full of prayers of saints and poets and prophets.

Prayer is one of the basics of Christian theology.

For years, I thought I knew all there was to know about praying. I talked to God, told Him what I needed and wanted, for myself and for others, added a few words of praise, some thanksgiving, and closed with the words, "in Jesus' name, amen."

Stop sign.

Prayer finished.

In all those years, I never understood that prayer is so much more.

I never understood that "prayer requires that we deal

with God—this God who is determined on nothing less than the total renovation of our lives."[2]

I wasn't interested in a renovation project—those are usually timely, costly, inconvenient, and at times painful.

I was interested in quick fixes by the Great Fixer of All Things Broken and Besieged.

Like most Christians I knew, I didn't understand that prayer is more than a monologue, more than a diatribe.

I didn't understand that prayer is a dialogue. It is "the great art of conversation with God."[3]

Never do we need both conversation and renovation more than when life is a mess.

Life-Giving Refreshment

My friend Anita is a missionary in Albania. During her last visit home, she told me about Brikena, a young Albanian woman who is in the Dallas area studying for a Masters degree in finance. Brikena needs some companionship, Anita said, a mentor. Was I interested? I love meeting new people, learning about other cultures, so I agreed.

I was a little nervous before Brikena and I met for dinner the first time. How good is her English, I wondered? How hard would I have to work to make myself understood, to understand her? What would we talk about?

In the first five minutes of conversation, I realized Brikena's English was as good as mine. We discovered we loved the same books, the same authors. Her intellect was sharp, her vocabulary amazing, and her humor contagious.

She told me about growing up under communism, about being an atheist in a family with Muslim roots, about university life in Albania, about becoming a Christian and living in fellowship with other university students who were learning to love Christ and each other as one body.

She told me how they celebrated Christmas together as first generation Christians after the repeal of communism, when, for the first time in their lives, and their parents' lives, worship was free and safe. Their holiday celebration lasted for days as they reveled in the joy of Christmas. For hours, days, they talked and sang and planned how, as the first Christians in their country to celebrate Christ's birth, they would create the traditions that would mark the celebration of this holy day for generations to come.

"So, how did you celebrate Christmas this year in the States?" I asked her over dinner one night.

Brikena shrugged, grinned. "I got drunk."

I laughed so hard I choked.

"It's true!" Brikena said, laughing and pounding on my back. "It was so sad. I was so alone—even with my host family. Because there was no conversation. Nothing to talk about, nothing to say. So, I drank wine, got drunk, and went to bed."

When I stopped laughing about the outrageous picture I had in my mind of this brilliant, godly young woman alone and drunk on Christmas Day, I apologized. Brikena shrugged again.

"It's okay. It's crazy, I know. But I was so dry, so empty inside, I just wanted to be numb."

Then she broke into a huge smile.

"Talking with you, having conversation, it's like after you've been thirsty for a very long time, and then you get a cool drink of water and it tastes so good."

I think I cried when she said that.

Tonight we meet for dinner again—tonight and every Wednesday night. We talk more than we eat. We laugh and share stories and sometimes we "problem solve" and brainstorm about how to work through challenges and difficulties. We compare our takes on new writers and books.

When we finally walk away from our half-eaten meals, we are full. Because we have partaken of great conversation.

We have mused, questioned, waited for answers; sometimes we really don't want answers, we just want to pose the questions, shape the thoughts, imagine the possibilities. Sometimes all we want to do is listen without pressure to answer, to respond. Sometimes all we want is to be spoken to.

And it occurs to me: This is what prayer is like, when it's real, when it is the "art" that God intended it to be.

By prayer, we join the great relational drama of the Trinity. We dine and converse with the triune God who spoke a word and galaxies exploded into light, who spoke and the earth appeared.

By prayer, we enter the conversation enjoyed by the Trinity, where the Father, Son, and Holy Spirit design the events of the cosmos and plan the rise and fall of sovereignties in our little world.

Through prayer, we speak, we listen, we answer.

"Amen" is not a stop sign. It is the signal for us to make the voice of God our total focus. It is the signal for us to begin listening, to hear God's words of comfort, to learn how He wants to renovate us, shape us, redeem us; it is the signal for us to prepare to answer Him with obedience and trust.

It is the signal for us to pause and recognize, with awe and humility, that we have been invited to sip the sweet wine of communion. We are invited to take into ourselves life-giving refreshment. Without it, we will remain thirsty and dry.

Crying Out

Emilie Griffin wrote that it is "important to begin where you are."[4]

It sounds simplistic, obvious. But how often have we agonized over how to begin? Do we sit and shape a prayer, adding words, subtracting them, editing to make sure God will not misunderstand?

What do you say to this God who already knows every thought in your head, every word before you speak it (Psalm 139:4)?

We can only begin where we are. If we are hurting, we begin there. If we are confused and angry, we begin there.

We begin where David begins in Psalm 6, crying out, begging for mercy, for healing, for God to pay attention to what is happening in our lives and make a difference for us.

I'm in anguish here, Lord. I'm in agony! How long do I have to endure this? David is saying.

He reasons with God: *If I die, I won't be around to tell how great You are.*

He whines to God: *I'm worn out!*

He pleads with God: *Mercy!*

Always, he is praying.

He has entered the sacred fellowship of the Trinity; He has joined his voice in conversation with the Father, the Son, and the Holy Spirit.

This is no place for pretence.

This is hard for us, isn't it? We are people who are used to pretending. We prevaricate, manipulate facts and feelings, hoping to coerce others, anyone, to get the outcome we think will best suit our needs. We plan our words to get the maximum effect, whether they are true or not. We aren't used to gut-level honesty with anyone, much less with God.

But prayer requires us, above all things, to be honest.

And so, we *have* to cry. We *have* to moan and groan and whine. We *have* to question. We are allowed to let our imaginations run amok. Listen to David, in misery and terror: "If you don't come through for me, Lord, my enemies will be on me like a lion! They'll tear me to pieces, shred me like cheap fabric, and no one will be there to rescue me!" (Psalm 7:2, paraphrase).

This is where we are when catastrophe strikes—desperate, terrified, imagining the worst.

We can pretend we're okay, and pray something fake and religious sounding, try to summon up a positive mental attitude, as if that would have some kind of power of its own to make things right. Or we can be honest, pray what is true, and pray from where we are.

David showed us how to pray from the pit of despair. He showed us what it looks like to be honest and direct with God. He showed us how to cry out our pain and fear to God.

And when we have finished with our crying out, when we're weary and empty of words and energy, our praying is not finished. David showed us that the conversation we call prayer is just beginning.

His Territory, His Voice

Henri Nouwen wrote that for too many of us, far too often, prayer is a monologue, not a dialogue. We often avoid what feels like a "mental wandering into the unknown."[5]

We line up our requests, list them on paper if we have to, and recite them to God. When nothing supernatural or extraordinary happens quickly, in response, we wonder where God is.

We wonder if we have prayed "right." Have we said

the proper words, intoned with just the right inflection? And so we sign up for another seminar on prayer or read another book about it. But real prayer requires us to wander into that unknown territory of the transcendent God whose ways aren't ours, whose thoughts aren't ours. We don't know what He intends for us, not for today, not for this hour. We don't know how He is going to work things out for our good, even though that is what He has promised. He isn't going to unfold the map and show us what comes next, or how we're going to get there.

In prayer, we have to settle down into mystery, and it's not a comfortable place for us. We want to get around it, get past it. We want to find a route to peace that doesn't have to go through regions we are unfamiliar with.

Maybe there's a formula for prayer that will trigger instant, deliberate, observable action on God's part. If we can just figure it out, put our hands on it, maybe we can get God to do what we're asking. Maybe we can speak the magic words that will unlock God's power and direct it to our problems.

Maybe we can make prayer work.

Here's great news: God is *always* at work for us, in us, and in the world around us. We don't need to find words, or formulas, or systems to unleash His power. As the psalmist wrote, "He stands at the right hand of the needy one" (109:31). We don't need to figure out a vocabulary that will persuade Him, or manipulate Him, or coerce Him into helping us, or healing us, or rescuing us. He promises to help us. He knows we are weak. He knows we often don't know how to pray, what to say, how to say it. "But the Spirit himself intercedes for us with groans that words cannot express" (Romans 8:26).

Our inarticulate groans harmonize with the divine agony of the Spirit, as He pleads for us with the Father. Our needs have been noted, our requests heard—the voice of God Himself has joined with our whispering, our roaring, our whimpering. How can we not rest in quiet confidence?

It is time now to listen. To hear. To remember that this is a conversation, not a monologue. To believe that God has something to say to us. Nothing is more important than hearing Him.

As Francois Fenelon prayed, "O eternal and omnipotent Word of the Father, it is you who speak in the depths of our soul."[6]

Listening

Look again at Psalm 6. David has groaned and moaned in honest desperation. You can see him worn out with tears. He is drained. His body is limp, his heart empty of everything except pain. Sorrow has sapped all the strength from his soul and his body. He falls on his bed, too weary to keep his eyes open.

Watch what happens next. Energy bolts off the page as David says, "Away from me, all you who do evil, for the LORD has heard my weeping. The LORD has heard my cry for mercy; the LORD accepts my prayer" (Psalm 6:8–9).

How does he know this? What has happened between verses seven and eight? What has happened since David wrote that he was weak, hardly able to lift his head because of the pressure of his enemies? What has happened to prompt him to say, "God heard me, God accepted my prayer, and He will fight for me"?

Here's what I think happened: David listened.

In the moments, maybe hours, that David lay on his bed, empty of words, wandering the unknown, he listened to God's side of the conversation.

Literal words?

Maybe.

Sometimes God does that for us. He speaks in our souls with words that we know could only have come from His Spirit, and we are stunned, overwhelmed. The weight of it, the glory of it wraps around us, swathing us in love, and fear is chased away. We aren't afraid of anything, or anyone.

More often, God's words are those we have read and heard and memorized over time. They are the words that Jacob heard, that Moses heard, that Joshua and Gideon heard. Words recorded for us, with the proof of the centuries behind them, telling us that God is good, God is loving and powerful and wise and always with us; that He is sovereign and unchanging. They are words in the Gospels, in the Epistles, words that teach us, encourage us, correct us, and comfort us. Jesus told us His Holy Spirit would remind us of His teaching and guide us in truth and counsel us (John 16:13).

Sometimes God's side of the conversation comes to us through His people, our friends who know God and have heard from Him in their own tough times. They speak the words we need to hear, and we are energized, revived. They share with us the comfort they received from God, and we are made brave (2 Corinthians 1:4).

Sometimes His message is a whispered reminder of His presence, or the Spirit's urging to trust. But always, there is the Word. Always, He speaks. Because that's what prayer is: conversation with God, two-way conversation.

A dialogue, not a monologue.

Michael Yaconelli wrote:

> If we truly want to hear God, if we truly want to hear
> Him speak, then we need to take time to savor Him.
> To immerse ourselves in our Father and bask in the

intoxicating presence of God's speaking voice—
this is prayer. Prayer is savoring God.
Prayer is *immersing* ourselves in His presence,
hearing Him with all our senses.[7]

Hearing God is easier if we listen with childlike faith,
if we are "willing to be naïve."[8]

Simplicity and Familiarity

Fenelon said of God," It is with babes alone that You are
wholly unreserved." He advises the Christian:

Talk with God with the thoughts of which your heart
is full. . . . Tell Him without hesitation
everything that comes into your head,
with the simplicity and familiarity of a little
child sitting on its mother's knee.[9]

David wrote of this kind of childlikeness—his own
(Psalm 131). This great king visualized himself as a child,
held and quieted in the arms of a mother.

We probably know David better than any other bibli-
cal character because he spilled his soul onto paper for us.
And when he wrote that he became still and quiet, we
know that often quietness came only after he wore himself
out with wrestling and writhing. We know that when he
said he did not concern himself with great matters, often
that was exactly what David did.

Read the Psalms and hear him ask "Why, God?" and
"How long, Lord?" Why do the cruel kings seem to be the
victorious ones? Why are idiots and fools prospering
while good people are suffering? Why does God even care
about the creatures He made?

I'm good at this kind of questioning too. I grab hold of a matter and look at it from every angle, measuring it, weighing it, trying to find an answer, a solution. I go round and round with it until I'm not only confused, I'm dizzy.

It's a common sport in this twenty-first century, isn't it?

Life is complicated. Beyond the basic issues that challenge us in the course of a day, we live with scientific discoveries and technological breakthroughs that bring into question concepts of right and wrong our grandparents never imagined, apart from the occasional fantasy stirred by a Ray Bradbury novel. Reverse time only one generation, and who could have guessed the national and global political complexities that would meet us in the newspaper every morning?

Never has the world been so dangerous, and our lives so chaotic.

Never have Americans felt so threatened, so despised, so helpless within the world community.

Our only hope for soul peace, for wisdom, is found in becoming like a child.

Like David, we have to let go of the wrangling and the circling. We have to relax into the arms of God. Like David, we have to settle down into the relationship—not of an infant who can't be held without demanding to be nursed—but into the relationship of a weaned child who asks nothing but the comfort and companionship of the loving parent.

David settled into the place where he could listen without being preoccupied and distracted by the sharp edges of his appetites.

Can we do this?

Can we stop twisting in God's arms, like a nursing baby that can't be held without demanding the breast?

Can we settle into the warmth of God's love, like a

child that is weaned, and be satisfied with nothing more than His presence?

Can we lean back on His chest, without demanding answers? Solutions? Without demanding *anything*?

David said that is the place where he found peace.

That is where he was able to hear God's side of the conversation.

That is where he heard words of hope.

And it was enough.

Isn't hope the one thing we all want above everything else? Hope that God will give us wisdom and discernment for the difficult decisions that face us; hope that God will give us courage to do what is right and holy; hope that God will be there for us when we're opposed, when we're frightened; hope that God will heal us and protect us and see us through.

It's not the kind of hope that wishes for rain tomorrow but has no way of knowing for sure. It's hope that means "confident expectation."

David was confident of God. He wrote:

> *We wait in hope for the LORD;*
> *he is our help and our shield.*
> *In him our hearts rejoice,*
> *for we trust in his holy name.*
> *May your unfailing love rest upon us, O LORD,*
> *even as we put our hope in you.*
> —PSALM 33:20–22

Do we know His name? Do we know Him intimately, as our "Abba," Daddy—our Father who is acquainted with all our ways, whose love for us is immeasurable?

If we know Him as the compassionate Father that He is, if we are familiar with His goodness and His power, we can rest against His heart in simplicity and childlike trust. Wrapped in love, we can listen to what He wants to say to us.

Answering

We cry out.

God responds.

We listen to His assurances, His directives, His counsel.

Now it is our turn to answer God.

This is where the conversation begins to resemble a renovation project.

God has laid out the truth for us. He has shown us a blueprint for building us into the people He wants us to be. He has shown us that He can use this catastrophe, this messy situation that has us on our knees in prayer, to shape us into the likeness of Christ.

"*All* things serve you," wrote the psalmist—not just the pretty, pristine things of life; not just the pleasant, successful endeavors—no! *All things!* (119:91, italics added).

Let yourself consider that for a moment. Let the hugeness of it settle into your mind: Almighty God is not diminished by the messes we encounter—not the ones we invite in, the ones we stumble into; not the ones others force upon us. His majesty isn't suddenly tarnished because we failed, or fell, or were abused and misused. Nothing is too big, or too bad, too good, or too grand to serve the purpose of God for us, for our joy, and for His glory. He will use anything that enters our lives, anything that intrudes, bringing joy or pain, pleasure or grief. He is big enough and powerful enough to turn it all into gold.

Whatever it is that breaks our hearts, His hands are strong enough to wring the shame out of it. He can turn our dirge into dancing, our weeping into singing. He can show us how to find peace and real joy.

Will we let Him use this painful thing, this life-shattering event, as a way of renovating us, forming in us a beauty of character we never imagined? Will we answer Him with humility and worship?

Will we let the voice of God direct us?

Or will we be driven by our appetites and directed by self-will?

We cry out. We listen as God responds.

We answer with our lives, opening ourselves to the work He wants to do in us, for us, through us.

This is what prayer looks like.

This is how prayer is lived.

This is how conversation with God becomes a kind of renovation project.

Sweet Living

Nearly four hundred years ago, Brother Lawrence was a cook in a French monastery. He washed pots and pans, baked bread, swept floors. No grand life for a man of God. When poor health forced him out of the kitchen, he worked as a cobbler, repairing sandals. The joy and simplicity that characterized him made him an enigma even among the godly monks who shared his life as a Carmelite. A prioress who knew him well described him as one who was "known by God and extremely caressed by Him."[11] Of himself, Brother Lawrence said:

> For me the time of action does not differ from the
> time of prayer, and in the noise and clatter of my
> kitchen, while several persons are together calling for
> as many different things, I possess God in
> as great tranquility as when upon my knees
> at the Blessed Sacrament.[12]

For Brother Lawrence, every moment was an opportunity to talk to God, to listen to Him, to answer with faith and obedience.

He called it "practicing the presence of God."

The apostle Paul called it praying without ceasing (1 Thessalonians 5:17).

He would have agreed heartily with Brother Lawrence's testimony that "there is not in the world a kind of life more sweet and delightful than that of a continual communion with God."[13]

Brother Lawrence built his spiritual life on this truth: that God is the Most High, most Holy One, worthy of all worship and adoration. He refused to let his mind be preoccupied with anything less than the sweetness and goodness of God. If other thoughts intruded, he made it his habit to quickly return his thoughts to God. He made it his life's occupation to be preoccupied with God's presence, talking, listening, answering with childlike trust.

It sounds daunting, doesn't it?

Is it possible to live in such a way in our modern world? Always thinking on God—praying without ceasing? Trusting utterly, with simple childlike faith?

What does it look like to be caressed by God, to be connected to Him, heart-to-heart, so that His closeness is as real, His voice as clear and welcome as the voice of a trusted friend?

Ask someone who prays.

Ask Erin.

Coming Close

Erin played her last concert with the Phoenix Symphony a few weeks ago. They performed a favorite of hers, Mussorskey's *Pictures at an Exhibition*—she knew it well and loved playing it. At the close of the concert, the maestro left the podium and walked to Erin, took her hand to help her out of her chair. While the audience rose to a standing ovation, he presented Erin with flowers and kissed her cheek.

So ended the career of a young woman who, as a child was considered a musical phenom, a prodigy. For more than two-thirds of her life, Erin studied, practiced, and worked tirelessly, determinedly, to win a seat in the string section of a symphony orchestra.

It's all over now.

Erin is now, officially, on permanent disability.

Her viola lays in its case.

She uses her meager energy to be a mother to her children and wife to David. She has nothing left over.

But the music isn't gone.

Erin hears the voice of God singing over her. She knows she is loved.

She knows that somehow, someway, God intends only good for her.

She is praying about what life is going to look like from now on. She is praying about the adjustment to a new kind of "normal." The pump surgically implanted in her abdomen dispenses pain-killing drugs into her spinal column. Most days, it isn't enough. The side effects are nausea, headaches, and exhaustion.

"Normal" for Erin means checking out the sidewalks at a local mall. Will her wheelchair cross the cobblestones without jarring her and triggering pain on those days when she can't walk?

"Normal" means summoning enough strength to bathe twin three-year-olds before having to lie down and rest; it means trying to figure out how to get five-year-old Darin to school on a day when she can't sit in the driver's seat because the pain is too severe.

It means planning every step, every activity, every family event around pulsing, pounding pain that at times can drop her to her knees. It means more doctors' appointments in a month than most people have in a span of years.

It means reconfiguring her entire life.

"We're praying about what that's going to look like for our family," Erin said recently. "We've got some decisions to make about where to live, how to situate ourselves to ask for help, how to know what's best for us. Changes are in store for us."

Erin prays a lot.

She cries out to God.

She listens too.

"I keep turning off the radio and getting off the phone because I really want to hear God's voice," Erin wrote me. "I don't want to do anything God doesn't want me to do."

For Erin, life is "exciting, yet scary, all in the same breath."

She is wandering "unknown territory," but she knows she is not alone. Her Father is with her, and she is willing to do whatever He says.

She is answering God with intent to obey.

Erin humbles me. She speaks with certainty about the goodness of God.

And she speaks with honesty about the questions, the unknowns.

She speaks of God with affection and trust.

"There are so many ways that God has shown His grace to us," Erin told me.

After a recent doctor's visit, she wrote, "I just love it when God provides a knowledgeable doctor!"

Erin understands what it means to be close to God.

So does my friend Beth.*

Beth's adult daughter recently disclosed that she had been molested as a child. Beth was devastated.

"It's over now, Mom," her daughter said. "It was a long time ago and I've been in therapy. But I thought it was time to tell you."

My friend couldn't forgive herself for not knowing, even though her daughter did not hold her responsible. She couldn't forgive herself for not being in the right place at the right time to protect her little girl, even though her daughter had long ago made peace with that fact and had spoken words of forgiveness and affirmation to her.

Beth couldn't stop tormenting herself with images and regrets. She couldn't stop the flow of tears. She began withdrawing from friends, from ministries that she had loved, from all but her closest family members.

Months passed, and still Beth found no peace.

Finally, one Sunday night, weary of the weight of it all, she collapsed on the floor, cradled her head, and wailed before God.

"You've got to help me, Lord," she begged. "I can't bear this sadness. It's destroying me. It's too big for me. Help me, Lord! Help me!"

Beth cried from the bottom of the pit.

And then she listened.

Silence greeted her. The torturing voices of accusation were quiet. No more shrieking in her soul. She heard only the quietness of peace as God's presence enfolded her with sweet stillness.

Moments earlier, her heart had been racing, trying to outrun pain and the banshee-wail of guilt. Now, it was calm, at rest.

*not her real name

Moments earlier, the deepest sorrow she had ever known had pressed hard and heavy on her soul. Now, she felt lightness.

Beth stood up slowly, as though testing this newfound airiness. Would her feet remain on the floor, or would she find herself floating? Her heart seemed free and weightless.

The only words she heard were the words she spoke in answer to God: "I'll take it, Lord! I'll take this gift!"

She called me a few days later to tell me what God had done in response to her prayer.

"I have to accept this joy God gave me. I can't explain it, but it's mine," she said. "He took the heaviness and darkness out of my heart, and I'm not going to question it. I'm going to live with this new joy."

Days later, Beth learned that a team of believers, her daughter's friends, had been on their knees that Sunday night, praying for her, praying that God would give her release and relief from the burden of guilt and sorrow.

Beth was overwhelmed yet again.

Weeks later, the lightness had not given way. Now months later, she still cannot suppress it. Her soul refuses to be weighed down.

Joy has returned. And Beth has returned to the ministries she loved.

Her life has been renovated.

Through conversation with God.

Glory Strength

More than two thousand years ago, Paul had a conversation with God about you and me. He prayed for us, and for all the followers of Jesus who would walk this earth before God shuts down history and brings us to heaven, our truest home.

We pray that you'll have the strength to stick it out over the long haul—not the grim strength of gritting your teeth but the glory-strength God gives. It is strength that endures the unendurable and spills over into joy, thanking the Father who makes us strong enough to take part in everything bright and beautiful that he has for us.

—COLOSSIANS 1:11–12 THE MESSAGE

Paul, with his tortured and scarred body, probably understood better than anyone that catastrophe would intrude into our lives. That none of us would be immune. That we would be called to endure the unendurable. But bruised and bleeding and clattering in chains, he witnessed the reality of God's strength that spills over into joy.

That encourages me.

I'm always heartened by the testimony of God's people who have suffered and found joy and comfort in the Shepherd's arms.

These are people who have lived through messy divorces, failed businesses, and violent physical traumas. They have lost spouses to tumors, children to drugs, careers to downsizing, and ministries to scandal. They have spent time with doctors and lawyers, judges and juries; they have been in churches and recovery groups and counselors' offices and funeral homes. And they have found Jesus there with them. They have heard His voice and felt His touch and seen evidences of His power and experienced His strength in ways I can only envy.

These are people whose lives have revealed to me secrets about God that no one else could whisper in my ear.

In humble submission, they have accepted the truth of Jesus' words when He said to expect sufferings of all kinds. "He, the Christian's model, was the man of sorrows, and his best people throughout the ages have always suffered the most."[14]

The great and excruciating sufferings of God's "best people" dwarf the small ouches of my life, yet their testimony is that suffering brought understanding; that there is a "grace of catastrophe" they never would have chosen, but having experienced, never would have missed: deep knowledge of God, sweet communion with Him, and what Paul describes as "glory strength."

Pure Gladness

Peter Kreeft poses an interesting question to this matter of suffering: Would you rather not have been born?

> Looking back at your life from the point of view of
> eternity, God's point of view, was it all worth it? Do
> you accept it, with all its suffering, as a package deal?
> Or would you exchange it for a womb,
> not to have been born?[15]

Go ahead—ask the question of yourself. Ask it of others who, like you, have had to endure tough times and pain; at times, suffocating pain. We all agree—we are glad to have been born. We are glad to have had this gift of life, even though it comes accompanied by pain.

What matters then, for all of us, is what we do with our pain.

Will we let it draw us into the heart-sweet intimacy that Christ desires to share with those He calls friend and beloved?

Will we open ourselves to receive the immeasurable portions of Himself that God wants to pour into His saints?

When catastrophe intrudes into our lives, will we let His love and gentle mercy and compassion change us and reshape us, molding us into His image?

George MacDonald wrote, "Grace is anything to make the heart glad with pure gladness."[16]

When God has picked us up, rocked us in His arms, and whispered His love words, sadness is transformed into gladness. We are glad to have been born; we are glad to have been born again.

We are glad to have had this opportunity to make the acquaintance of so great a God as the one who calls Himself El Shaddai—the God who is enough for us. He is enough for any crisis we will ever encounter; enough for satisfying every hunger, every yearning that can be found in the human heart.

We are glad to be here, in this place, where suffering rips at us and sorrow shoves its way into our lives, because it is here that our souls have learned to commune with God, our Father. It is here we have discovered the reality of His "glory strength."

We are glad to be here, in the midst of catastrophes and messes.

Yes, we are glad, because it is here, even here, in this story full of light and dark, that Jesus has taught us more about His gentle love and fierce devotion than the easiest times and most pleasant circumstances could have taught us.

Through the grace of catastrophe, a door has opened to us, and we have stepped into a kind of intimacy with the triune God that, until our hearts were scarred by His love, until His mercy ruined us, we didn't even know how to imagine.

Our sufferings have enabled us to know Almighty God.

And for that, we will be eternally glad.

 TRACKING GRACE

HE HIDES IN DIFFICULTY. HE HIDES IN SUFFERING. HE
HIDES IN POVERTY. HE HIDES IN FAILURE, AND HE HIDES
IN THE STORIES OF OUR LIVES. WHATEVER OUR CIRCUM-
STANCES, WHATEVER THE STATUS OF OUR LIVES, GOD IS
PRESENT, WAITING FOR US TO LEARN FROM HIM IN THE
SHADOWS AS WELL AS IN THE LIGHT.[17]

—MICHAEL YACONELLI

Be joyful in hope, patient in affliction,
faithful in prayer.

—ROMANS 12:12

1. If prayer is conversation with God, how would
    you rate your conversation skills?

2. What does it mean to you to think of prayer as
    "wandering the unknown"?

3. What has been your experience of listening to
    God in prayer?

4. In what ways have you felt closeness or intimacy
    with God through prayer?

5. In what ways has prayer renovated your heart?

6. What is your response to the idea of "gladness" and "glory strength" in the context of suffering?

7. Take a moment to identify where you are right now: Are you in the "shadows" or "in the light"? Thinking about the idea of God "hiding," what would it look like for you to seek Him?

8. In a prayer, or a poem, or a simple paragraph, record something you think God wants you to know about Himself in order to make you glad and strong.

NOTES

Chapter 1: Life in the Midst of Mess

1. A. W. Tozer, *That Incredible Christian* (Harrisburg, Pa.: Christian Publications, 1964), 27.

2. Charles Colson, *Loving God* (Grand Rapids: Zondervan, 1983), 218.

3. A. W. Tozer, *The Divine Conquest* (Wheaton: Tyndale, 1950), 4.

4. A. W. Tozer, *Knowledge of the Holy* (New York: Harper and Brothers, 1961), 10.

5. Eugene Peterson, *Living the Message* (New York: HarperCollins, 1996), 181.

6. John Piper, *The Legacy of Sovereign Joy* (Wheaton: Crossway, 2000), 70.

7. Calvin Miller, *Into the Depths of God* (Minneapolis: Bethany House, 2000), 144.

8. Henri Nouwen, *With Burning Hearts* (Maryknoll, N.Y.: Orbis Books, 1994), 49.

9. Mariano DiGangi, ed., *A Golden Treasury of Puritan Devotion* (Phillipsburg, N.J.: P & R Publishing, 1999), 96.

10. Karen Mains, *The God Hunt* (Downers Grove, Ill.: InterVarsity, 2003), 137.

11. Peterson, *Living the Message*, 190.

Chapter 2: God's Unfathomable Ways

1. Jean-Pierre de Caussade, *The Sacrament of the Present Moment* (New York: HarperCollins, 1982), 65.

2. Dallas Willard, *Renovation of the Heart* (Colorado Springs: NavPress, 2002), 133.

3. G. K. Chesterton, *Orthodoxy* (New York: Random House, 2001), 11.

4. Job 4:18–19 THE MESSAGE.

5. Michael Yaconelli, *Dangerous Wonder* (Colorado Springs: NavPress, 1998), 43.

6. Amy Carmichael, *Edges of His Ways* (Fort Washington, Pa.: Christian Literature Crusade, 1955), 84.

7. Amy Carmichael as quoted by Elisabeth Elliot, *A Chance to Die: The Life and Legacy of Amy Carmichael* (Grand Rapids: Revell, 1987), 342.

8. Willard, *Renovation of the Heart*, 125.

9. Ruth Bell Graham, *Collected Poems* (Grand Rapids: Baker, 1998), 186.

10. Tozer, *That Incredible Christian*, 38 (see chap. 1, n. 1).

11. Ibid.

12. Millie Stamm, *Be Still and Know* (Grand Rapids: Zondervan, 1978), reading for May 4.

13. Frederick Buechner, *Listening to Your Life* (New York: HarperCollins, 1992), 221.

14. John Piper, *Desiring God* (Sisters, Ore.: Multnomah, 1986), 50.

15. John Piper, *The Misery of Job and the Mercy of God* (Wheaton: Crossway, 2002), 72.

16. Ibid., 66.

17. Willard, *Renovation of the Heart*, 133.

18. Job 13:15 and Job 16 (my paraphrase).

19. Brennan Manning, *Reflections for Ragamuffins* (New York: Harper-Collins, 1998), 45.

20. Jean-Pierre de Caussade, *Abandonment to Divine Providence*, trans. John Beevers (New York: Doubleday, 1975), 64.

21. Blaise Pascal, *Mind on Fire*, ed. James Houston (Minneapolis: Bethany House, 1997), 95.

22. Willard, *Renovation of the Heart*, 129.

23. Henri Nouwen, *The Only Necessary Thing* (New York: Crossroad Publishing, 1999), 60.

24. Eugene Peterson, *A Long Obedience in the Same Direction* (Downers Grove, Ill.: InterVarsity, 2000), 63.

Chapter 3: Realm of the "Totally Other"

1. Julian of Norwich, *Revelation of Love*, trans. and ed. John Skinner (New York: Doubleday, 1997), 13.

2. Peter van Breeman, *The God Who Won't Let Go* (Notre Dame, Ind.: Ave Maria Press, 2001), 10.

3. Buechner, *Listening to Your Life*, 200 (see chap. 2, n. 13).

4. Peter van Breeman, *The God Who Won't Let Go*, 27.

5. George MacDonald, *Discovering the Character of God*, ed. Michael R. Phillips (Minneapolis: Bethany, 1989), 29.

6. C. S. Lewis, *Mere Christianity* (Westwood, N.J.: Barbour and Co., 1952), 40.

7. Peterson, *Living the Message*, 327 (see chap. 1, n. 5).

8. Lewis, *Mere Christianity*, 36.

9. Chesterton, *Orthodoxy*, 97 (see chap. 2, n. 3).

10. Manning, *Reflections for Ragamuffins*, 297 (see chap. 2, n. 19), and Manning, *A Glimpse of Jesus* (New York: HarperCollins, 2003), 129.

11. Peter Kreeft, *Making Sense out of Suffering* (Cincinnati: St. Anthony Messenger Press, 1986), 143.

12. Manning, *Reflections for Ragamuffins*, 305.

13. Larry Crabb, *Pressure's Off* (Colorado Springs: Waterbrook, 2002), 123.

14. Piper, *Desiring God*, 222 (see chap. 2, n. 14).

15. Kreeft, *Making Sense out of Suffering*, 143.

16. Teresa of Avila, *Ecstasy and Common Sense*, ed. Tessa Bielecki, (Boston: Shambhala, 1996), 76, 115.

17. *A Golden Treasury of Puritan Devotion*, 149 (see chap. 1, n. 9).

18. Gerald Sittser, *A Grace Disguised* (Grand Rapids: Zondervan, 1995), 180.

19. van Breeman, *The God Who Won't Let Go*, 25.

20. C. S. Lewis, *Screwtape Letters* (New York: Macmillan, 1967), 22.

21. *A Golden Treasury of Puritan Devotion*, 95.

22. Sam Storms, *The Singing God* (Lake Mary, Fla.: Creation House, 1998), 9.

23. Soren Kierkegaard, *The Prayers of Kierkegaard* (Chicago: University of Chicago Press, 1956), 14.

Chapter 4: The Basis for Everything

1. Crabb, *Pressure's Off*, 204 (see chap. 3, n. 13).

2. Peterson, *Living the Message*, 198 (see chap. 1, n. 5).

3. Tozer, *That Incredible Christian*, 65 (see chap. 1, n. 1).

4. Oswald Chambers, *My Utmost for His Highest* (New York: Dodd, Mead & Co., 1935), 322.

5. Oswald Chambers, *Still Higher for His Highest* (Grand Rapids: Zondervan, 1970), 250.

6. Mains, *The God Hunt*, 153 (see chap. 1, n. 10).

7. *A Golden Treasury of Puritan Devotion*, 15 (see chap. 1, n. 9).

8. Eugene Peterson, *Leap over a Wall* (New York: HarperCollins, 1997), 39.

9. Buechner, *Listening to Your Life*, 277 (see chap. 2, n. 13).

10. Richard J. Foster and Emilie Griffin, eds. *Spiritual Classics*, (New York: HarperCollins, 2000), 7.

11. Henry van Dyke, Public Domain.

12. Frances Radley Havergal, Public Domain.

13. Manning, *A Glimpse of Jesus*, 54 (see chap. 3, n. 10).

14. George MacDonald, *Knowing the Heart of God* (Minneapolis: Bethany House, 1990), 80.

15. *A Golden Treasury of Puritan Devotion*, 15.

16. Willard, *Renovation of the Heart*, 130 (see chap. 2, n. 2).

17. MacDonald, *Discovering the Character of God*, 78.

18. Willard, *Renovation*, 53.

19. Lewis, *Screwtape Letters*, 55 (see chap. 3, n. 20).

20. Peterson, *Living the Message*, 308.

21. Jeanne Guyon, *Experiencing the Depths of Jesus Christ* (Auburn, Maine: SeedSowers Books, 1975), 18.

22. Brother Lawrence, *The Practice of the Presence of God* (North Brunswick, N.J.: Bridge–Logos Publishers, 1999), 95.

23. Peterson, *Living the Message*, 295.

Chapter 5: The First Necessary Truth

1. *Golden Treasury of Puritan Devotion*, 14 (see chap. 1, n. 9).

2. Peterson, *Living the Message*, 221 (see chap. 1, n. 5).

3. Sam Storms, *Pleasures Evermore* (Colorado Springs: NavPress, 2000), 136, 139.

4. Ibid., 137.

5. Ibid., 139.

6. Peter Kreeft, *Fundamentals of the Faith* (San Francisco: Ignatius Press, 1988), 239.

7. George MacDonald, *Proving the Unseen* (New York: Random House, 1989), 79, 106.

8. Willard, *Renovation of the Heart*, 51 (see chap. 2, n. 2).

9. Tozer, *Knowledge of the Holy*, 33 (see chap. 1, n. 4).

10. Buechner, *Listening to Your Life*, 316 (see chap. 2, n. 13).

11. John Bunyan, *The Acceptable Sacrifice* (Shippensburg, Pa.: Destiny Image, 2001), 5.

12. J. C. Ryle, *Holiness* (Darlington, England: Evangelical Press, 1997), 37.

13. Spiros Zodhiates, ed., *NIV Hebrew-Greek Key Word Study Bible* (Chattanooga: AMG Publishers, 1996), 1507.

14. Ryle, *Holiness*, 34.

15. Gary L. Thomas, *Seeking the Face of God* (Eugene, Ore.: Harvest House, 1994), 67.

16. Buechner, *Listening to Your Life*, 274.

17. Bunyan, *The Acceptable Sacrifice*, 74.

18. Kreeft, *Making Sense out of Suffering*, 143 (see chap. 3, n. 11).

19. Brother Lawrence, *Practice of Presence*, 91 (see chap. 4, n. 22).

20. Kreeft, *Fundamentals of the Faith*, 227.

21. Mark D. Roberts, *Jesus Revealed* (Colorado Springs: WaterBrook, 1996), 82.

22. Bunyan, *The Acceptable Sacrifice*, 76.

23. Ibid., 80.

Chapter 6: Our Safe Refuge

1. Arthur Pink, *The Attributes of God* (Grand Rapids: Baker, 1975), 46.

2. Tozer, *Knowledge of the Holy*, 74 (see chap. 1, n. 4).

3. Piper, *Desiring God*, 48 (see chap. 2, n. 14).

4. Tozer, *Knowledge of the Holy*, 56.

5. Pink, *Attributes of God*, 19.

6. Tozer, *Knowledge of the Holy*, 57.

7. Jan Winebrenner, *Steel in His Soul* (Chicago: Moody, 1985), 36.

8. Tozer, *Knowledge of the Holy*, 1.

9. *A Golden Treasury of Puritan Devotion*, 13 (see chap. 1, n. 9).

10. Tozer, *Knowledge of the Holy*, 67.

11. *The Lord of the Rings: The Two Towers*, New Line Cinema, Wingnut Productions: 2002, based on the book by J. R. R. Tolkien.

12. Kreeft, *Making Sense out of Suffering*, 108 (see chap. 3, n. 11).

13. Philip Yancey, *Reaching for the Invisible God* (Grand Rapids: Zondervan, 2000), 95.

14. Peterson, *A Long Obedience*, 79 (see chap. 2, n. 24).

15. *Spurgeon's Sermon Illustrations*, comp. and ed. David Otis Fuller (Grand Rapids: Zondervan, 1942), 126.

16. C. S. Lewis, *The Problem of Pain* (New York: HarperCollins, 1996), 33.

Chapter 7: Nothing's Changed—It Never Will

1. *A Golden Treasury of Puritan Devotion*, 9 (see chap. 1, n. 9).

2. Guyon, *Experiencing the Depths*, 28 (see chap. 4, n. 21).

3. John Piper, *Don't Waste Your Life* (Wheaton: Crossway, 2003), 73.

4. Francois Fenelon, *Fenelon: Talking with God*, (Brewster, Mass: ParacletePress, 1997), 58.

5. Guyon, *Experiencing the Depths*, 86.

6. Thomas Watson, *All Things for Good* (Carlisle, Pa.: Banner of Truth Trust, 2001), 29.

7. Fenelon, *Fenelon: Talking with God*, 142.

8. C. S. Lewis, *The Weight of Glory* (New York: HarperCollins, 1980), 41.

9. Ibid., 39.

10. A. W. Tozer from *The Best of Tozer*, comp. Warren Wiersbe (Camp Hill, Pa.: Baker, 1980), 26–27.

Chapter 8: Between the Paws of the True Lion

1. Brenda Waggoner, *The Myth of the Submissive Christian Woman*, (Carol Stream: Tyndale, 2004), 138.

2. Lewis, *The Problem of Pain*, 33 (see chap. 6, n. 16).

3. J. I. Packer, *Knowing God* (Downers Grove, Ill.: InterVarsity, 1973), 73–74.

4. *A Golden Treasury of Puritan Devotion*, 40 (see chap. 1, n. 9).

5. Willard, *Renovation of the Heart*, 52 (see chap. 2, n. 2).

6. J. I. Packer, *Your Father Loves You*, comp. and ed. Jean Watson (Wheaton: Harold Shaw Publishers, 1986) reading for September 1.

7. Lewis, *Problem of Pain*, 47 (see chap. 6, n. 16).

8. Ibid., 34.

9. C. S. Lewis, *The Last Battle* (New York: Collier Books, Macmillan Publishing Co., 1970), 107.

10. Carmichael, *Edges of His Ways*, 123 (see chap. 2, n. 6).

11. Peterson, *A Long Obedience*, 64 (see chap. 2, n. 24).

12. Nouwen, *With Burning Hearts*, 94–95 (see chap. 1, n. 8).

13. John Piper, *A Godward Life*, (Sisters, Ore.: Multnomah, 1999), 290.

14. Arthur Pink, *The Sovereignty of God*, (Grand Rapids: Baker, 2002), 19.

Chapter 9: Body Heat

1. Michael Yaconelli, *Messy Spirituality* (Grand Rapids: Zondervan, 2002), 76.

2. Jan Winebrenner, *Intimate Faith* (Nashville: Warner Faith, 2003).

3. John Eldredge, *Waking the Dead* (Nashville: Thomas Nelson, 2003), 192–193.

4. Yaconelli, *Messy Spirituality*, 15.

5. Henri Nouwen, *The Inner Voice of Love* (New York: Image Books, Random House, 1998), 7.

6. Dietrich Bonhoeffer, *Life Together* (New York: Harper & Row, 1954), 26.

7. Henri Nouwen, *Reaching Out* (New York: Doubleday, 1975), 153.

8. Ibid., 153.

9. Bonhoeffer, *Life Together*, 20.

10. Ibid., 19, 23.

Chapter 10: The Great Art

1. Peterson, *Living the Message*, 136 (see chap. 1, n. 5).

2. Eugene Peterson, *Answering God* (New York: HarperCollins, 1989), 12.

3. Ibid., 5.

4. Emilie Griffin, *Clinging: The Experience of Prayer* (New York: Harper & Row, 1984), 6.

5. Henri Nouwen, *The Way of the Heart* (New York: Ballantine Books, Random House, 1981), 56, 57.

6. Fenelon, *Fenelon: Talking with God*, 58 (see chap. 7, n. 4).

7. Yaconelli, *Dangerous Wonder*, 87–88 (see chap. 2, n. 5).

8. Griffin, *Clinging*, 5.

9. Fenelon, *Fenelon: Talking with God*, 58.

10. Ibid., 2.

11. Brother Lawrence, *Practice of Presence*, 75 (see chap. 4, n. 22).

12. Ibid., 16.

13. Ibid., 83.

14. Kreeft, *Making Sense out of Suffering*, 142 (see chap. 3, n. 11).

15. Ibid., 88.

16. MacDonald, *Proving The Unseen*, 93 (see chap. 5, n. 7).

17. Yaconelli, *Dangerous Wonder*, 75 (see chap. 2, n. 5).

SINCE 1894, Moody Publishers has been dedicated to equip and motivate people to advance the cause of Christ by publishing evangelical Christian literature and other media for all ages, around the world. Because we are a ministry of the Moody Bible Institute of Chicago, a portion of the proceeds from the sale of this book go to train the next generation of Christian leaders.

If we may serve you in any way in your spiritual journey toward understanding Christ and the Christian life, please contact us at www.moodypublishers.com.

"All Scripture is God-breathed and is useful for teaching, rebuking, correcting and training in righteousness, so that the man of God may be thoroughly equipped for every good work."
—*2 TIMOTHY 3:16, 17*

MOODY
PUBLISHERS

THE NAME YOU CAN TRUST®

THE GRACE OF CATASTROPHE TEAM

ACQUIRING EDITOR
Mark Tobey

COPY EDITOR
Ali Childers

BACK COVER COPY
Laura Pokrzywa

COVER DESIGN
LeVan Fisher Design

COVER PHOTO
Getty Images/Gallo Images, Roger De La Harpe

INTERIOR DESIGN
BlueFrog Design

PRINTING AND BINDING
Versa Press, Inc.

The typeface for the text of this book is
Fournier